Don't Let Them Stop You – It's Personal!

How to Navigate Complex Environments and Still Make Progress

Angela R. Morris MSc.

Don't Let Them Stop You – It's Personal!

DON'T LET THEM STOP YOU – IT'S PERSONAL!
How to Navigate Complex Environments and Still Make Progress

Copyright © 2023 by Angela R. Morris MSc.

All rights reserved. No portion of this publication without permission may be reproduced, stored in a retrieval system, or transmitted in any form or by any means – scanned, electronic, mechanical, photocopied or recorded without the author's written consent as it is strictly prohibited.

Excerpts and links may be used, provided full and clear credit is given to the author with specific reference to the original content.

If you would like to use the author's book for short quotations or personal group study, this is permitted other than for review purposes. However, prior written permission must be obtained on request by emailing the author at angiestrategymorris@gmail.com.

Paperback ISBN Number: 9781739660772
e-book ISBN Number: 9781739660789

Publisher: Authentic Worth
Website: www.authenticworth.com

Authentic Worth Publishing is bringing worth back into you through storytelling and book writing!

Don't Let Them Stop You – It's Personal!

Dedicated to my children, grandchildren, and future generations to come. You are all awesome!

Don't Let Them Stop You – It's Personal!

Foreword

Is it possible in the first half of the 21st century to live without fearing what other people think? Angela Morris says not only is it possible, but it's necessary to live fearlessly. Read this important book if you want to know how!

Eric Collins
Host of Channel 4 Reality Business Show; *The Money Maker*
Serial Entrepreneur.

Don't Let Them Stop You – It's Personal!

Contents Page

Introduction	Page 1

Chapter 1   Page 5
What About You?

Chapter 2   Page 18
Families; Who Needs Them?

Chapter 3   Page 49
Friends; Simply The Best?

Chapter 4   Page 59
Significant Others – What's Love
Got To Do With It?

Chapter 5   Page 90
Bouncing Back From A Setback Is Possible

Chapter 6   Page 107
A Word About Spiritual Leaders

Chapter 7   Page 121
Back To You!

Chapter 8   Page 135
How Do I Self-Reflect? (Bonus Chapter)

Conclusion   Page 138
References   Page 139
Further Reading   Page 143
Resources   Page 145

Don't Let Them Stop You – It's Personal!

Introduction

As the clock struck 12 midnight, I burst into tears without any warning! Why? Where was I? I was on an aeroplane coming back to England from Jamaica, and as I travelled home, I had turned 60 years of age in the air! I wasn't crying because I was upset. Not at all! Quite the contrary! I took a moment to go to the toilet cubicle to give God thanks that I had made it thus far and what an incredible journey it had been. Not tears of sadness but tears of joy that this girl from the council housing estates of Battersea in London England, could over the odds and lead a remarkable life, and was still living to tell the tale! An air steward then announced my birthday over the airwaves and gave me a complimentary bottle of champagne which I thoroughly enjoyed. Nice one!

So, who am I? I am a woman of colour born to Jamaican parents in 1962. I arrived in a world of "No blacks, no Irish, no dogs." Not that I knew any of this, I was too busy fighting my own health war of pneumonia and then double pneumonia from my birth to 6 months. According to my parents (and trust me, the story was told many times) I had visited death's door more than once as a young baby and survived against all odds! Can you imagine in those days, regardless of how poorly your children were, due to your economic circumstances, your father to go to work knowing that by the time they got home, their baby may have expired! Hard to imagine, isn't it? Well, that's exactly what my father had to do!

My name is Angela Rosemarie. It was given to me on my deathbed by my parents by order of the nurses who did not expect me to survive long birth. They told my parents to call the priest, which they promptly did, and as a result, I have no godparents!

Well, here I am, 60 years later writing a book to encourage you to make great use of your time here on earth. The first step towards this is to understand your right to have a personal life and to be able to make choices that you are personally happy with.

Don't Let Them Stop You – It's Personal!

I recognise that in my storytelling, I am not alone. We are all presently here having survived all sorts of situations and I am sure some of you may have even more dramatic stories than mine.

My disclaimer: I am not a therapist, but I do understand the principles of therapy and have obtained a Master's Degree in Applied Psychology. And no, I can't read minds! Just thought I would put that in before you ask! I can however decode personality profiles for which no Psychology qualifications are required. It's a helpful skill to have in my industry as a business coach. Actually, it's helpful if you are involved in any public facing service.

Enough about me for now. I want to focus on you by asking some questions that may help you think about yourself as you go through the book:

- Do you ever feel like you are losing yourself? By that, I mean do you have a strong sense of who you are?

- Are you able to quickly identify the environments that make or break you; those that add value or are a liability? Those that keep you in the status quo?

- Have you ever felt like you are being suffocated or smothered? Not in a literal sense (but it may feel like that), but an overwhelming feeling of not having control over your life?

This book is written to those individuals who feel invariably lacking in strong identity, stuck, powerless or trapped in a world of other people's opinions. I understand that each individual owns their experiences and for each person it will feel different based on how they process their life encounters. I am not in the business of minimising anyone's life experiences! If you feel you are doing fine and just want to get this book to help out a friend, that's good too!

Don't Let Them Stop You – It's Personal!

However, for the one who feels they aren't fulfilling their full potential (notice I didn't say *reaching?* That sound's tiring!) and you know there is more to be achieved, there remains an underlying feeling of being trapped in a world not of your creation, but someone else's. There can be many reasons why this happens, and, in this book, we will explore who *those people* are. While some people don't let anyone get in their way of progression of life, some of us don't find it easy to bulldoze our way through the myriad of other people's opinions and thoughts of us, which, in turn impacts our decision-making skills.

Maybe this isn't you. Maybe you are a "bulldozer!" You really don't care what people think; your life is your own and nobody can tell you what to do and how to do it! Maybe you know people like that, and you look on with a mixture of admiration and envy. You wish you could be that person or…maybe you think they're being selfish! If you think the latter, then the "bulldozers" would say "tough!" These personalities will not allow their peace of mind to be disturbed! We possibly all have 'bulldozer' moments (normally at the end of our tether from contorting ourselves of everyone's expectations), but how to find a balance? That is part of this book's exploration.

So big up and congratulations to the "bulldozers" as I call them. They are a force to be reckoned with and you might get some consolation from knowing that they are the minority (hope you feel a bit better now!)

As for the majority of us, we usually make our decisions based on a plethora of influencers (who may not even know that they are influencers, and we in turn, may not recognise are being influenced) and that's just life. These "influencers" are the people who raised us, lived with us, played with us, loved us, taught us, worked with us, and even prayed with us. They are the people who have been in and out of our lives, sometimes coming and going without any fanfare, but who at the same time have deposited thoughts, suggestions, and ideas without us even noticing!

Don't Let Them Stop You – It's Personal!

This book is titled "Don't Let Them Stop You! – It's Personal." You are about to embark on a journey of discovering who the people or situations are that get in the way of your personal growth and what you can do about it.

Lastly, I understand that we all have different ways of taking information, and I would like this to be a positive experience for every reader, so along the way, I've taken the liberty to insert the opportunity for you to make some notes (if you wish) which may help you to process your life's journey.

* "Bulldozers" – I made that term up to describe certain characteristics of individuals. You don't have to become one or claim yourself as one! Have I ever met one? Yes, I have. I know several actually; they do phenomenal things. Primarily, they don't overthink things, and as a result leap over barriers. On the other hand, they can be incredibly self-centered and don't think about the impact on others! But don't let that stop you from having a go yourself! When reading this book, consider when you might have some "bulldozer" moments for yourself!

Happy reading and may your life go from strength to strength!

Don't Let Them Stop You – It's Personal!

CHAPTER 1

What About You?

The beauty of life is to be able to detach yourself from environments that don't add any value to your life! *"What about me?"* I hear you ask (in varying tones of voice). Well, this book is all about you becoming the person you really want to be (with some inspiration and motivation from me of course!) and losing the fear of people's opinions. Yes, this can really happen, and yes, you can be the sole director of your own life, no longer a prisoner of other people's fears and insecurities. Is that a bold claim? I prefer to say it's a necessary, liberating and a very possible statement.

While this is most certainly about YOU, can I share a couple of important nuggets I have learned that may also be useful to you? A lot of our struggle rests on not knowing the power of setting boundaries for our lives.

Have you ever wondered why you exist? I am not going to give you an answer, I am going to say that these thoughts and questions are quite common to all people.

This leads me to the point that we have quite a lot in common; you and I; yes, we really do. Not sure what these things may be? Then let me list a few things:

- We all have a finite amount of time on the earth
- We all have relationships with people on some level
- We all want to get on in life (whatever that looks like to you)
- We all want to be accepted for who we are on some level
- We all want to live as peaceably as life (or people) will allow us to!
- We all want to manage any dramas with as little drama as possible (drama kings and queens are excluded!)

Don't Let Them Stop You – It's Personal!

Do you see? None of the above is relative to colour, class, culture, religion or however we choose to identify ourselves. This is about doing our best to live our lives with a sense of being a whole person in every way. There is a commonality.

So, who or what is stopping YOU from achieving this? Sometimes the answer is clear as black and white, sometimes it's grey, and sometimes it's a multicoloured affair!

When I first went into therapy (yes, I did and yes, it was great!) it was quickly determined that I hadn't set any boundaries for my life. Really? How could this be? On the surface, I came across as confident, articulate, and assertive. I was a Pastor, and I also had a good career for goodness sake! How wrong can we be about any individual, including ourselves? During with process, my eyes were opened in a way that gave me another perspective to life, in other words, it took a while to sink in. More on this later…

Having survived the turbulent first 6 months of life (see introduction), I would love to tell you that life gets easier after that! Well…we all must grow, and in doing this, we find that life gets more complicated. Just think for a moment about the people we must contend with throughout our life's journey. Even if that comprises mainly of parents, siblings, friends, educators, spiritual leaders, and work colleagues. Phew! That's still a lot of people, all of whom can have a varying degree of influence over how we see life and how we interact with everyone, including ourselves. The journey of life can be arduous at times, but only *at times,* not all the time.

Perhaps we look through lenses that have been tainted by our own experiences or teachings? Or just not recognising smoke and mirrors because we are busy producing our own? (*Ouch!)*

How we perceive (or see) ourselves is vital to our development and growth as individuals. If you find it difficult to describe yourself, don't be alarmed. Again, it's all perfectly normal (unless you have done lots of work in this area); however, there will always be the outlier, the exception to the rule. Have you ever met someone who is a great communicator in a very small group who then falls apart

Don't Let Them Stop You – It's Personal!

when asked to speak or present in front of a crowd? Nerves? Possibly, but it could be because they don't see themselves as the same person in every setting. You might say that many people are like that, and you would be correct.

I strongly believe one of the keys to not letting people (thoughts, opinions, whatever.,) stop you is to be as authentic as you possibly can be in every situation. Is this possible? Yes. Does it come at a cost? Yes, but what of value doesn't have a cost? I am not talking about money here, although that could be a factor; however, I am referring to perhaps the consideration of what would be the price of being liberated emotionally or mentally.

Many years ago, I attended a meeting and heard a standout statement which the speaker said, I found at that time to be profound was, "deliver me from the expectations of people!"

Does that statement resonate with you in any way?

What a great response the audience had to that statement; after all, the average person understands exactly what this person meant and were touched that someone was bold enough to say it. The speaker was unable to give any strategies because it was highly likely that they were still trying to work it out themselves! One cannot; however, doubt the sentiment of that loaded statement.

I will share these snippets for the simple purpose of motivating you (to encourage you to engage in therapy if you feel you need it and not feel bad about it), and perhaps you might recognise a yourself from the examples.

- Do you feel the need to be delivered from the expectations of people?

- How do you know if you are working under boundaries that you have set or that others have set for you?

Don't Let Them Stop You – It's Personal!

- How is *"value'* determined in your life? What does *"Added Value"* look like to you?

Here are some questions to ask yourself:

- Do you ever feel under compulsion to take actions others have requested (or pressured) rather than do them out of your own free will?
- Who do you feel is dictating the narrative of your life? You? Family? Friends?

- Are you speaking from your own thoughts and voice? Or do you hear the voice of someone else? (They could be alive or deceased; it can still be powerful!)

Yes, it's a lot to think about, but don't let that put you off at all. I feel that we don't spend enough time reflecting or thinking, as we are too busy taking actions, some of it non-productive.

When looking at how to set boundaries for our lives, we need to reflect (just a bit) on how you have arrived at this point.

Firstly, let's look at what the definition of a boundary is:
The definition of boundaries means "anything that marks a border." It's a real or imagined line that marks the edge or limit of something or the limit of a subject, principle, or relationship.

Boundaries is such a powerful word and I confess that I thought I understood what it meant, but I didn't understand how that word should be applied within our everyday lives and within various relationship settings.

Let me put this scenario out to you and you can respond based on your thoughts and opinions:

Don't Let Them Stop You – It's Personal!

- Finding yourself in a situation where you feel the need to disclose personal information when you don't really want to!

- Allowing others to "interrogate" you about matters that are personal or confidential to yourself or others (and again, you really don't want to!)

- You feel you have no choice but to answer their questions or even agree with them!

IF YOU NEED PERMISSION, PLEASE ALLOW ME TO GIVE YOU SOME: You are allowed to "hold something back" for yourself and there is no need to feel obligated to share all your personal information with everyone or anyone for that matter!

Repeat after me out loud: **"I will go about MY daily affairs without fear of what people may think!** Do this 3 times a day, every day (like medicine) and see what happens!"

The word "transparency" is used and often banded around in so many different settings, but not every setting is being transparent (or telling all) appropriate.

At this juncture I would like to about culture…

As a woman of African Caribbean origin, I was brought up in a Jamaican culture where secrecy was highly valued. Those of you from my era and culture will understand the saying "don't tell anybody your business!" I think these instructions were passed down generationally, basing itself in superstition and fear. We were not allowed to question why it was important not to tell anyone your business; we were not from the generation that asked our parents "why?" We just did as we were told! The problem with that is, if everything is a secret, how can you know when to speak?

Don't Let Them Stop You – It's Personal!

Fast-forward 50 years and we are now in the era of what some may call "oversharing." Nothing is secret and nothing is private! There is no escaping it folks; the age of digital media is here in full force in the Western world and all we can do is manage it the best way we can (I know that makes me sound old fashioned, and that can't be helped when you reach my age!)

My question is (and this is still about you); can you discriminate between what is:

Personal information?

What is personal information?

- Your age
- Gender
- How many brothers and sisters you have
- Your favourite band
- Your favourite food
- What pets you have
- The name of your pet
- Your opinion about an important issue

What is private information?

- An individual's name, signature, address, phone number or date of birth
- Medical status and records
- Credit information
- Employee record information
- Photographs
- Internet protocol (IP) addresses

What is confidential information?

Any information that is intended to be kept secret.

Don't Let Them Stop You – It's Personal!

What is secret information?

"Not meant to be known by others"
In other words, a secret is something kept hidden or unexplained.

I hope this makes things clearer if you weren't sure. I want you to be able to think about how you share information about yourself and who you share it with based on YOUR choices. I will remind you throughout this book that YOU DO HAVE CHOICES!

Let me be clear; you can share whatever you want with whoever you want, but this should always be on your terms and not because you feel you have "no choice." I am also very mindful that within various cultures, it would appear rude for you not to subject yourself to a barrage of questions from the "elders" of your communities (and I am including family members here). For some of you, it will mean that you will have to muster up some courage to give a response that doesn't leave you feeling stripped of dignity or feeling "less than." So, can I give you a couple of statements you can make?

- It's okay to say 'I can't disclose any information about that.'
- It's okay to say 'I am not ready to talk about that.'
- It's okay to say 'I can't discuss this right now as I am still processing things myself.'
- If putting the word "sorry" at the beginning of the sentence makes you feel better.

The alternative is to give in and share your personal stuff (which is giving away some of your power) or make up elaborate stories to put them off the scent. When you do that; however, you are not setting boundaries, you are leaving the gates open. You will leave others with the impression that it's okay to ask you whatever you want, but it's not okay if you don't want to!

I get it. You don't want to upset anybody, but at what cost? At the cost of you being upset by others instead. I did say it will take some

Don't Let Them Stop You – It's Personal!

courage on your part. Why? Because only YOU can do this, and no-one can do it for you!

I am not going to tell you that it's going to work first time around. In fact, some people may become more insistent and not respect the boundary you are wanting to set. That's when you need to dig deep and repeat the same statement. I will tell you this, when you start doing this, people will think twice about crossing boundaries! Let them call you whatever! Rude? Disrespectful? Yes, these labels may be applied to describe you; however, you know the truth (and so do I) that you want people to respect your right to have some privacy.

Here are a few things you can do in addition to help yourself:

Stop oversharing – This an act of revealing an inappropriate amount of detail about one's personal life. It may take some discipline, especially if you do this with everyone you meet. Remember, people need to earn the right to learn personal things about you and you are not necessarily respected when you give too much information about yourself having met someone briefly. I used to do this a lot. I did not understand it was due having a lack of boundaries and my churchy background encouraged us to be "transparent."

Stop trying to hide from people – It's not a contradiction to the previous point. You do not need to apologise for living your life. Just go about your business without fear of what people think. A good friend of mine said "Opinions are like noses…everyone's got one!" Think about things from a practical perspective, other than gossiping what will anyone really do?

Recognise that in the long run, people respect you more when you set boundaries in your life. They may be a bit taken aback at first by your new approach, and some may even try and push back, but if they do this, then this must act as an alarm bell for you, that they do not honour the person that you are.

Don't Let Them Stop You – It's Personal!

Those friends or family members who truly respect you and your decision-making will understand and back off!

Can I talk? On a personal note, I used to be afraid of shutting down conversations or questions people would ask me about my personal life. I didn't realise it was okay not to share personal information under the guise of being "transparent." I came from a world where you were expected to confess every misdemeanor to the elders (in this instance, it was the church setting), and only then could you repent and move on. Not knocking this approach if it works for you; however, if it doesn't, then that is quite a different matter!

When I separated from my husband, I was overwhelmed with feelings of guilt and shame for many years. My decision wasn't about him, it was about my growing up and my life moving in a direction which was different to my younger years. What was I most fearful of? What others would think of me. I was afraid of their opinions. One of the reasons for these fears was because I was in a position where I was always supporting people, trying to rescue people from their situations, and now I was someone who needed help. I saw this as a climbdown from my somewhat lofty place and worse still, I didn't really believe that anyone from my circle could support or help me.

Now don't get me wrong, it is lovely to help and support people (I still enjoy doing this now in a different capacity); however, I have learned the hard way that balance is something you must strive for as this can be a cover for not attending to your own issues. I did have to draw some boundaries with people that I knew which involved me telling them that I am not discussing my personal business and not feeling obligated to. What happened when I did this? Nothing; they respected my decision and left it alone. I have also come to realise that any news-breaking story concerning your life transitions, is only as exciting until the next bit of exciting news (or salacious gossip) about someone else comes out. In other words, nobody cares as much as YOU think they do!

Don't Let Them Stop You – It's Personal!

Back to talking about YOU, how about a bit of reflection?

Although we are talking about how other people can make us feel, have you thought for a moment how YOU might make other people feel too?

Are you someone who is quite nosey? Do you find that you cross boundaries and ask intrusive questions? Or do you wait for people to share on a voluntary basis?

What about all this "rescuing" that you do? How does that make you feel (you can be honest here; I won't tell anybody!)

Do you ever feel taken for granted? Feel you can't say "no" to certain people or to anyone? Do you feel drained but keep going regardless, not taking a break?

These emotions can take place in particular environments or in all environments you relate to. If it sounds like a nightmare being in that situation, you would be right; it is!

I am all about quick wins. I can't help it, it's just the way I think. Whenever I feel a bit overwhelmed with a mammoth task, I remember the old riddle: How do you eat an elephant? The answer: Piece by piece. I brought this up because when addressing matters such as these, the temptation can be to put the book down and forget about transformation. You could end up with the feeling of "it's long!" (As the young people would say), but I am asking you nicely to not run away, either literally or figuratively, but to come under the spotlight and make this all about you!

So, I will ask you again what about you? Who are YOU?

STOP! Before you start writing, you are not a career or an occupation; you are a vibrant living being! A person with a variety of characteristics, behaviours, and personalities. I would like you to visualise yourself somewhere nice. Perhaps on a beach, in a forest, in a nice country house or penthouse suite! It is from this place that

Don't Let Them Stop You – It's Personal!

I would like you to think about who you are and write down what words come to mind:

_____

_____

_____

_____

_____

If I were to ask your friends and family about YOU, what would they say? Well, that's a bit of a trick question, in as much as I don't really care what they think; I care about what YOU think about you!

What descriptions come to your mind?

_____

_____

_____

_____

_____

Hopefully, you were not too hard on yourself and that you had some positive things to say about yourself.

So just how special are you? Before you answer, I want you to think about how many millions or even billions of sperm had to beat the race to impregnate your mother's egg! Now, a new study shows that even though the fastest and most capable sperms reach the ovum first, it is the egg that has the final say on which sperm fertilizes it.

Don't Let Them Stop You – It's Personal!

I want you then to consider how much DNA you need to be you. Not sure? Out of the various combinations to become you, it was possible. The human DNA sequence consists of nearly 3 billion DNA base pairs and the order of these base pairs is nearly identical from person to person:

- You are not a biological mistake
- You arrived on this planet against the odds
- You survived your family and their antics
- You survived your negative experiences
- You survived all traumas you experienced at the hands of others
- You are reading this book
- You are here!

YOU ARE GOING TO BE FREE!

Don't let anyone tell you that you not special! You are a survivor, despite all that you have experienced in your life, up to and including this very moment. Many have not made it to tell the story that you will soon be able to tell and here you are reading this book.

I understand and applaud those of you who have worked very hard to get to where you are. You may even feel that you are constantly fighting to prove yourself and your worth. That takes a lot of energy and is not sustainable over the long term.

For those of you who are truly embedded in the social media age, there is a lot of information circulating out there. People telling you who you can and can't be, or who you should be, but what about what you think? Yes, I am asking you; what do you think about YOU?

Many people are uncomfortable talking about themselves, and that maybe because we have been taught not to do that. Does it all seem

Don't Let Them Stop You – It's Personal!

a bit self-indulgent to talk about yourself? Were you made to feel that you are being self-centered even to consider talking about your feelings, accomplishments, or perhaps your disappointments?

I get it; for me, it's part cultural, part religious upbringing, and part family construct. I am of Jamaican origin – don't judge me!
Back to the question of who are YOU?

No need to answer in this very moment (although I must say I think you are rather fabulous); however, as we go through this book, it will be wonderful for you to use the notes and reflection spaces to write down your personal thoughts. And don't worry, I won't tell anybody!

I will ask you to commit along the way. Not to anyone other than yourself! You deserve some commitment after all you have been through up to this stage of your life. Committing to yourself may be a totally new concept; however, this will help you when it comes to setting boundaries to protect yourself from unwitting people who may wish to take advantage of you.

When you commit to yourself (and I mean really commit!) this will influence how we approach others and how we allow them to approach us! You will realise that you deserve to be treated with dignity and respect when the truth of being committed to yourself becomes your truth.

Don't worry if you don't get it all now; we shall get back to YOU later…

CHAPTER 2

Families; Who Needs Them?

Whilst there are exceptions to the rules, most of us were born into some form of family construct. We usually have at least a mother, possibly a father and possibly some siblings. In this chapter, we are going to explore family dynamics and how we can be impacted and influenced by our family.

I think people don't always know the power of the things they say to others, especially in the family setting! I have heard of parents who push their children down the career paths of THEIR choice, not the child's, and who have decided who their children can or cannot marry based on their own prejudices.

Because there are so many different settings in which child-rearing can take place, I am also quick to acknowledge that some of you may have been raised by your grandmother and/or grandfather as your parents for a multiplicity of reasons. Others may have been looked after by foster parents (sometimes one and sometimes a few!). For some, it may have been aunties, uncles or even big brothers or sisters.

I suppose the point I am making before we go into this chapter is that somebody, somewhere had a significant input in our lives which shaped and moulded not only how we see the world, but also ourselves. Whoever you claim, as your "mother", "father", or "siblings" etc., is entirely up to you. I do not know your life; you do. I don't want you to get bogged down in who you didn't have for family. We will go with the family you know, even if they are not your blood relatives.

I have deliberately made the distinction between male and female parents. The biological make-up of a woman is different to a male and this is dictated by our reproductive system and hormones. In most cases, the mother is the primary care giver (even if they do

Don't Let Them Stop You – It's Personal!

work outside the home), and usually there is some form of maternal bond.

A father can have a very close bond with the child, but it is not the same as the mother (remember what I said about hormones?). Unfortunately, it would appear that certain communities within our Western society does not want us as females to rest in our femininity. In some circles, to even acknowledge being feminine is looked down on!

As I go through each of the roles and their influences, I also want to make it clear that there are no absolutes in parenting and there are many ways to parent a child, some of which are great and some not so much. I would like you to try and read this section and reflect on YOUR experiences and not what your other family members may have experienced. This book is to help YOU, not other people (they can buy their own copy!) because in truth, we cannot understand someone else's experience; only our own.

Oh, just a second…

The subject I chose for my dissertation for my Masters was on the subject of Afro-Caribbean parenting. This was of great personal interest to me. I think it will be helpful to some of you if I interject a section here about parenting styles [1]. You may recognise your own experience of being parented below:

Parenting is a complex and multifaceted task which involves various approaches and styles. Different styles of parenting have been identified by researchers, each with its unique characteristics and effects on children's development. We will briefly explore four different styles of parenting:

    (1) Authoritarian
    (2) Authoritative
    (3) Permissive
    (4) Uninvolved.

Don't Let Them Stop You – It's Personal!

The *authoritarian* style of parenting is characterised by strict rules, high demands, and little flexibility. Parents who use this style tend to be controlling and rely on punishment to maintain discipline. Children in authoritarian families may feel that their opinions and feelings are not valued, and may be afraid to express themselves. They may also struggle with low self-esteem and have difficulty making decisions on their own.

In contrast, the *authoritative* style of parenting is characterised by warmth, responsiveness, and clear boundaries. Parents who use this style set high expectations for their children, but also provide support and guidance. Children in authoritative families tend to have high self-esteem, are more independent, and have better social and academic skills than their peers.

The *permissive* style of parenting is characterised by low demands and high responsiveness. Parents who use this style tend to be indulgent and have few rules. Children in permissive families may have difficulty following rules and may struggle with self-control. They may also experience anxiety and have difficulty making decisions on their own.

Finally, the *uninvolved* style of parenting is characterised by low demands and low responsiveness. Parents who use this style are often disengaged and neglectful. Children in uninvolved families may struggle with emotional and behavioural problems and may have difficulty forming healthy relationships with others.

It is important to note that these parenting styles are not mutually exclusive, and parents may use a combination of these styles depending on the situation and their children's needs. Moreover, the effects of parenting styles on children's development can vary depending on factors such as culture, socioeconomic status, and children's temperament.

It cannot be denied that parenting styles have a significant impact on children's development. The authoritarian, authoritative, permissive, and uninvolved styles are four distinct approaches that have different effects on children's self-esteem, social skills, and

Don't Let Them Stop You – It's Personal!

academic achievement. By understanding these styles and their effects, parents can make informed decisions about how to best support their children's growth and development.

So, let's dig in to our own parents, shall we?...

Our mothers

Interesting characters, aren't they? Just ask someone about their mother, and if you are observant within just a few moments, you will get a sense of that person's relationship with them (whether they are deceased or alive). Emotions range from total adoration spattered with some reality through to utter disappointment and even hatred in some cases.

And my point is?...

Our birth mothers became pregnant, and then carried us around for approximately 9 months, then brought us into a world in which we spent several years (and some) trying to work out how the world works and our place in it. If that wasn't challenging enough, all this took place without our express permission! Who are these people!?

Well, there is a type of "payback" for taking these rather giant steps of giving birth and keeping these children. Firstly, mothers usually get a lot of blame for a lot of stuff that happened to us that caused our lives to go wrong, and secondly, mothers have to take a lot of flak for who we have turned out to be or what we have now become (that usually happens when we don't feel things have gone in our favour).

On a positive side, when we are feeling good about ourselves, and have achieved our life dreams, we then give our mothers' lots of praise and will not have a bad word said against them (even if they were not very good; really). Think about the praise lavished on parents at award ceremonies! Should they pass away before we are tempted to immortalise them and paint them as picture perfect? It is at the point of death that we can choose to forget the difficult parts

Don't Let Them Stop You – It's Personal!

(or at least put those parts at the back of our minds) and focus on the good deeds they performed.

It used to be said that the mother set the temperature of the home with the inference that if she was happy, then life would be happy for everyone, and if she was not, then everyone would feel that too!

We are more aware than ever that life is full of different experiences including Domestic Abuse, Mental Health (with its many categories e.g., depression, borderline personality disorders, OCD, Bipolar, Schizophrenia, ADHD, and Autism), PTSD, Alcoholism and Child Sexual Abuse. In some circumstances, these experiences remain hidden or undiagnosed, making it even more challenging when looking after children who are thrown into the mix.

It may not be anything I have mentioned so far, but it could be something more practical such as mum always being at work when you were young, (or so it feels), leaving you feeling abandoned and uncared for.

Let's keep it real; in addition to the above, some mothers are very controlling! Depending on your culture of origin, they may want to get heavily involved in who you are to marry, or even want you to date who *they* believe is appropriate, not considering who *you* think may be appropriate. They may want you to study where *they* want you to study, not where *you* want to study.

In other words, there may be a smothering of your voice and opinions that exists in your culture, where you are expected to totally obey your parents, even when you are an adult. This is sometimes described as being respectful to your elders.

As we grow into adults, we can sometimes reflect on our mothers and realise that something was not "quite right" with them and with this recognition, we understand that their treatment of us was the best they could do with what they knew or understood about themselves. We might even feel that we have unfairly suffered the brunt of their issues. I have to say that in certain circumstances you would be absolutely correct. When you have crossed cultures or

Don't Let Them Stop You – It's Personal!

have had to straddle across your family culture and your society's culture, things become complex as you are mentally working out what now works for you and not just your parents. Coming to certain conclusions about how *you* feel, is the best way to live *your* life, then generate question of: What can you do about it?

1. You can't exactly go and fight her! (I definitely don't recommend this action for several reasons!)

2. You might be able to have a discussion with her face to face, over the phone or by letter. This could go really, really well or really, really badly. So, it's a 50-50 on this one. Sorry, I have to be honest! (There are no guarantees, especially based on which culture you were raised in; my black and brown people may decide to tread with caution here!). On the other hand, you might feel a "bulldozer" moment come over you, and feel better having expressed yourself and got some things off your chest!

3. You might want to read through this chapter, and at the end of it, decide if the process of healing is more about you finding your own peace, than trying to "dig it out" with them and getting them to acknowledge their failures!

Why is it difficult to get others to acknowledge their part in causing you distress or hurt? My answer is because as a rule, people don't like being made to feel guilty, even if they are!

A wise man once said: "It is easier for a man to find the blackest ant in the blackest dirt in the blackest of night, than for him to see his own faults." (Don't ask me who the wise man was; I honestly don't remember, but this is both powerful and true!)

Let's be honest, most of us love our mothers, but the reality is although they gave birth to us (or not), there are some truths we must face:

Don't Let Them Stop You – It's Personal!

- They (normally) want the best for you
- They don't always get you
- They have their own issues
- They want to live their lives again (through you)
- They don't always even understand themselves
- They are not necessarily good at communicating their feelings.

What is a mother's role?

I would say it's straightforward and complicated at the same time. Every mother will have their own definition of how they should raise their children. Much of this will be based on their own experiences and what they carry over from their experiences. I think it's true to say that much of motherhood will be based on what is called "culture-bound" experiences. For now, however can we agree on the following 5 duties at least in principle?

To love unconditionally – To love without any strings attached and not based on how good you are, or what you have achieved. Some cultures are better at this than others. For some, how much love you receive is directly linked to how proud you can make your parents! This can start from very young when the focus is on being good or well-behaved. This can create the "overachiever" in children who become adults, who drive themselves relentlessly to gain the approval of their parents, in some cases, even after those parents have died!

Score: ____

To care both physically and emotionally – To provide shelter, physical and verbal affection, a place of safety, good nutrition, and healthy diets. Taking some time to play with them and have some fun, making sure they have access to healthcare and medical care,

Don't Let Them Stop You – It's Personal!

making sure they have enough rest, being fair, and giving them a growing sense of independence.

Score: _____

To correct to discipline and train – Be an example and show, rather than just tell, redirect negative behaviours, give reasonable consequences for persistent negative behaviours, have time-outs (for both of you!), expect a level of naughtiness! It is unrealistic to not expect children to get up to mischief as they grow, experiment and test what works and what doesn't. After all, they are only little humans!

Score: _____

To build, to encourage and teach – Give them age-appropriate tasks and offer some choice and freedom (set some limits too!) Give them some space and don't smother them with your fears. Allow them to develop their own identity and do not try to recreate your life through them! (Also known as living "vicariously".) On a cultural level, this can be very challenging, as some parents dictate what careers they want their children to have before they're born and can remain very dogged in their decisions even when the child does not have an interest or aptitude for this "chosen" career!

Score: _____

To connect with your children and grow with them – Take an interest in their hobbies, be mindful of your own feelings, be open to hear their fears, concerns, dreams and hopes. Recognise that you may need to make some changes or adjustments to your own behaviours

Score: _____

Don't Let Them Stop You – It's Personal!

All of the above can be summarised as showing love. If these actions do not come from the heart, it is unlikely you can sustain it. Sure, you can do it as a one-off or for a couple of weeks, but you cannot truly love without giving of yourself (or did you think it was only about what you can get?)

A bit about love languages; bear with me please...[2]

If you haven't heard of this concept, then I strongly recommend you purchase some material on the subject. It has proven to be transformative in helping people in their relationships.
The underlining principle is to learn and understand a person's love language (there are some tests involved) which will in turn, help you to show love and also how you receive love.

Love is a complex emotion that can be expressed in many different ways. Some people express their love through words, others through actions, and still others through physical touch or gifts. These different ways of expressing love are often referred to as love languages, and understanding them can be the key to building stronger and more fulfilling relationships.

The concept of love languages was first introduced by Dr. Gary Chapman in his book "The Five Love Languages: How to Express Heartfelt Commitment to Your Mate." In this book, Chapman identified five main love languages:

1. Words of affirmation
2. Acts of service
3. Receiving gifts
4. Quality time
5. Physical touch.

Words of affirmation refer to verbal expressions of love and appreciation, such as saying "I love you," complimenting your partner, or expressing gratitude for something they've done. For

Don't Let Them Stop You – It's Personal!

people whose primary love language is words of affirmation, hearing these positive words can be incredibly validating and affirming of their self-worth.

Acts of service, on the other hand, involve doing things for your partner that show them you care. This might include cooking them a meal, doing their laundry, or taking care of a household chore they've been dreading. For people whose love language is acts of service, these actions can speak louder than words and show that their partner is willing to go out of their way to make their lives easier and more comfortable.

Receiving gifts is another love language that involves giving and receiving physical tokens of affection. For some people, the act of receiving a gift is a tangible reminder of their partner's love and thoughtfulness.

Quality time is another love language that involves giving your partner undivided attention and engaging in meaningful activities together. This might involve going for a walk, cooking a meal together, or simply spending time talking and connecting with each other. For people whose love language is quality time, these shared experiences can be incredibly important for building intimacy and connection.

Physical touch is a love language that involves the sensation of touch, such as hugging, holding hands, or cuddling. For people whose primary love language is physical touch, these sensory experiences can be incredibly important for feeling connected and loved.

It's important to note that everyone's love language is unique, and what works for one person may not work for another. It's also possible to have more than one primary love language, or to have different love languages in different contexts or relationships.

Understanding your own love language, as well as your partner's, can be incredibly helpful for building stronger, more fulfilling relationships. By knowing how your partner prefers to receive and

Don't Let Them Stop You – It's Personal!

express love, you can tailor your actions and words to better meet their needs and deepen your connection.

Love languages are a powerful tool for understanding and expressing love in all its many forms. By learning about and embracing the different ways in which people express love, we can build stronger, more fulfilling relationships and create deeper connections with the people we care about most.

Where do my mother and I stand in our relationship? Do I understand my mother's love language? Does she understand her own love language?

If you fundamentally agree, you could take the next step and score your mother's parenting skills between 1-10 (1 = Poor, 10 = Excellent). Wait!! Just before you do that, I want you to consider the following…

What might her upbringing have been like? What challenges may she have faced? Was she operating in survival mode? Did she have enough support? What fears has she tried to transfer to keep you safe?

Depending on their age, their behaviours could also be the effects of the menopause. As I said before, life is complex, and we only know other mothers from a particular angle!

Some of the questions I have raised may not be able to be answered (especially if you are from African-Caribbean culture where asking such questions would be considered rude!) even so, if you can observe and reflect on past behaviours, you could definitely pick some clues.

Okay, now you can score…

You can use the above categories to assess your own parenting (if you have children), and evaluate or ask an honest, yet kind relative or friend how you are doing.

Don't Let Them Stop You – It's Personal!

WHY DOES IT MATTER?

Not throwing any shade on anyone's mother and their parenting skills, but for you to start your journey to freedom, you will need to gain some insight into how you got here. I mean, in this position, (on a physical level, I think we all know how you got here!) Can we do anything about the past? Not the actions of the past, but I strongly believe we can understand more about who we are based on what we have experienced, especially in our formative years.

Take a moment and consider where you feel you are on life's journey and if what you are going through at this present time, is helping you go forward in life.

Some people are stuck in the past, but there are some people that keep moving forwards. We must learn something from the past. History teaches us lessons that are to be learned to stop us making errors in the future, where we can. We should be comfortable to make decisions. We might want to shut down ourselves emotionally, but there will be times where you must hurt to heal. I will give you the heads up that if you can't self-reflect, you are going to struggle.

We all need to do some reflection i.e., journaling, walking, travelling, revisiting books, watching a movie, communication, recording your voice, video recording on thoughts and reflections, observing the Sabbath (religious observance) etc. It helps us to remember where we have come from, who we are and reminds us of our identity.

In my time as a practitioner in the health and social care industry, I have spoken to young women who have become stuck in their mental health cycle due to their refusal (yes, I did use that word), to accept that life had dealt them a difficult hand, and they were landed with mothers who wouldn't or couldn't love them in the way they needed.

My heart goes out to them, as it is like having a prison sentence for a crime you didn't commit! If only they knew the power of acceptance, I know they could completely change their lives! Is it

Don't Let Them Stop You – It's Personal!

good to acknowledge any hurt that we feel as a result of our mother's lack of skills? Absolutely! Denial of feelings is never the healthy alternative to address any pain we feel. Will we be upset? Yes. Will we cry buckets of tears? Possibly. Will we eventually start to feel better? Most certainly.

A note for those who truly feel (or know) you have been abandoned and now struggle to manage your mental health:

> **The root of ones' mental health can be due to absence of maternal input or the presence of a maternal figure in your life.**

Sometimes, the basis of a relationship between a mother and father is unknown; also, the circumstances surrounding conception. A baby's arrival or conception can impact ones' mental health.

Did I mention that you need courage to go on this journey within this book? Apologies if I didn't! Yes, you will need some courage, but not a lot, just enough to face a few questions to find out exactly "who" is stopping you from becoming the person you *really* want to be.

DON'T LET THEM STOP YOU!

What 3 areas of life do you believe about your mother's relationship has impacted you the most?

1.

_____

_____

Don't Let Them Stop You – It's Personal!

_____

_____

_____

2.

_____

_____

_____

_____

_____

3.

_____

_____

_____

_____

What 3 promises do you want to make to yourself after reading this chapter? (I promise I won't look!)

1.

_____

_____

_____

Don't Let Them Stop You – It's Personal!

2.

3.

Our fathers

I recognise we are now living in an age where the family structure has changed a lot and, in many homes, (certainly in Western culture) there is no traditional "head of the house." Whereas, the role of the mother has more or well remained constant for decades, the role of a father has changed over the years from breadwinner, disciplinarian or protector. We are now able to identify a mixture of males who are single fathers, stay at home fathers, non-resident fathers or stepfathers, each position bringing its own style of parenting. How much influence your father has (had) is based on how present they have been in your pre-adult years and the generation you were brought up in.

Don't Let Them Stop You – It's Personal!

We are more aware of the subtly of mental health and how men address (or not) these issues. As I mentioned with the mothers, there can be similar situations with fathers where mental health is concerned, which have invariably had an impact on your life and relationship with him. The issues that I mentioned previously: Domestic Abuse, Mental Health, PTSD, Alcoholism and Child Sexual Abuse impacts males as well as females, however the effects may look different in men.

It gets even more complicated when you have a father who is trying raise you on his own, and maybe living with someone else who is not your mother. He ends up over or under compensating with you being the guinea pig (I doubt if actually he knows what he is doing, just playing it by the ear like the rest of us!)

What is the father's primary role?

I am mindful that there are lots of fatherless people in the world, and some may even argue; is there a position for a "lead" head of the house anymore regarding the men? We all need to acknowledge and respect different family structures, not negate one to lift up the other. Are we not all born from another human? Only a few were raised by wolves!

I will bring to your attention though; there are theories within parenting that an active and present father can instill confidence in their female children and that an absent father can have an impact to the degree that a woman doesn't know or appreciate her self-worth.

We must face the following truths with fathers:

- They (normally) are protectors
- They (normally) want the best for you
- They don't always "get" you
- They have their own issues
- They are not always able to express their emotions
- They sometimes want to live their lives again (through you)

Don't Let Them Stop You – It's Personal!

- They don't always even understand themselves

It's only fair that we score fathers too! (I hear you cry) and I agree. But just before we do that, can we just consider the following:

What might his upbringing have been like? What challenges may he have faced? Was he operating in survival mode? Did he have enough support? What fears has he tried to transfer to keep you safe?

To love unconditionally

To love without any strings attached and not based on how good you are, or what you have achieved. Some cultures are better at this than others. For some, how much love you receive is directly linked to how proud you can make your parents! This can start from very young when the focus is on being good or well-behaved. This can create the "overachiever" in children who become adults who drive themselves relentlessly to gain the approval of their parents, in some cases, even after those parents have died!

Score: _____

To care both physically and emotionally – To provide shelter, physical and verbal affection, a place of safety, good nutrition, and healthy diet. Taking some time to play with them and have some fun, making sure they have access to healthcare, and medical care, making sure they have enough rest, being fair, and giving them a growing sense of independence.

Score: _____

To correct to discipline and train – Be an example and show rather than just tell, redirect negative behaviours, give reasonable consequences for persistent negative behaviours, have time-outs (for both of you!), expect a level of naughtiness! It is unrealistic to not

Don't Let Them Stop You – It's Personal!

expect children to get up to mischief as they grow, experiment and test what works and what doesn't. After all, they are only little humans!

Score: ____

To build, to encourage and teach – Give them age-appropriate tasks, offer some choice and freedom (set some limits too!), give them some space and do not smother them with your fears. Allow them to develop their own identity and do not try to recreate your life through them! (Also known as living "vicariously.") On a cultural level, this can be very challenging as parents can dictate what they want their children's careers to be before they are born, and can remain very dogged in their decisions, even when the child does not have an interest or aptitude for this "chosen" career!

Score: ____

To connect with your children and grow with them – Take an interest in their hobbies, be mindful of your own feelings, be open to hear their fears, concerns, dreams and hopes. Recognise that you may need to make some changes or adjustments to your own behaviours!

Score: ____

Where do my father and I stand in our relationship? Do I understand my dad's love language? If you fundamentally agree, you could take the next step and score your mother's parenting skills between 1-10 (1 = Poor, 10 = Excellent). Wait!! Just before you do that, I want you to consider the following…

What might his upbringing have been like? What challenges may he have faced? Was he operating in survival mode? Did he have enough support? What fears has he tried to transfer to keep you safe?

Okay, now you can score…

Don't Let Them Stop You – It's Personal!

You can use the above categories to assess your own parenting (if you have children) and evaluate or ask a friend how you are doing.

What 3 areas of life do you believe about your father's relationship has impacted you the most?

1.
_____
_____
_____
_____
_____

2.
_____
_____
_____
_____
_____

3.
_____
_____
_____
_____
_____

Don't Let Them Stop You – It's Personal!

Siblings

You can't choose your siblings; they just come with the package of family. It is almost a privilege to have them and take them for granted! It's like they will always be there, until they are not.

Aside from this, parents are very good at labelling siblings in the family, and siblings are very good at embracing these labels (especially if it makes them look good!). It's a form of low-level stereotyping, one which makes the whole family a bit lazy when it comes to getting to know the individuals within the household.

An example of this is describing (or labelling) the children as:

- The smart or clever one
- The sensitive one
- The troublemaker
- The good on
- The sweet one
- The rude one
- The cheeky one.

The problem with this is that children subconsciously start to live up to their label. As adults, we don't always understand the impact of our words on children.

The challenge is that if you have embraced any labels (even the good ones), it takes away your capacity to see yourself outside of it, or your ability to form a different identity to what you have been given. We all need a sense of personal identity, I am not what you say I am, I am what I say I am!

I don't care how much people say whom you are like or what you are like. You must not embrace a false identity created or based on the opinions of others, or even your life experiences. You must find out who are and own it! I am raising this issue as many times as we are trapped in the description of our families from childhood. Again,

Don't Let Them Stop You – It's Personal!

this may be more prevalent in some cultures more than others. This can be both challenging as well as being annoying!

What do I mean?

For example, if you have been labelled as the good one, there is a subconscious pressure to live up to the expectation of always being good, and no-one is always good! The "good child" feels they always need to meet whatever is asked of them. They never feel they can express a refusal to a request. They tend to work hard at keeping their parent's love, and are fearful that any bad behaviour will meet their parent's disapproval. This puts in their minds that they always have to work hard for affection. If you're curious…I was the good one!

The child that has been given this label may seem happy-go-lucky at first, but they are inclined to hold in their feelings as they are too busy trying to meet the expectations of their parents and can end up holding onto their feelings and ultimately not express their emotions, which can have negative effects on their development. This may resonate with some of you.

We all know what negative labelling can do and we do not underestimate its power! Some of the saddest people in the world are living under the cloud of negative labelling and will tell you stories of how throughout their childhood, they were constantly told they would amount to nothing. Truly awful, yet not unsurmountable with the right support around you.

The good news is you no longer have to be a prisoner of anyone's label. What can you do? Peel it off and throw it away (metaphorically of course!) or you can write the label you were given on a piece of paper and burn it, then throw the ashes in the wind. Very therapeutic!

If you are an only child, the chances are that none of the above applies to you and that's okay!

Don't Let Them Stop You – It's Personal!

Between 1992 – 1993 our family was blind-sided by the sudden death of a brother and a sister. They were my half-siblings from both my mother and father, so they were related to each other through the marriage of my parents, but anyone who knows Jamaican culture knows that we don't do "halves", they are just siblings.

For 2 years, I walked around in a fog of grief. I couldn't make sense of what was going on. How could this happen to us, why did it happen to us? A God-fearing church going family? It's times like this when you realise you are not exempt from life's tragedies, irrespective of your beliefs.

It's all part of being human on planet earth, and some situations you cannot "pray" away; you just have to live through them. Losing your siblings makes you value whatever ones you have left! Even so, you cannot be held ransom by your brothers or sisters because they probably know you better than anyone (dare I say even your parents). They may know you well, but they are not you. They are not privy to the inner workings of your mind and the daily conversations in your head, nor are they living your daily life.

It's okay to feel an admiration, even a deep respect for them, but don't let their "greatness" in your eyes, get in the way of your progress. Did you know that your siblings can have a tremendous influence over your life's choices? Sometimes it's blatant e.g., "What are you dating them for?" or "I wouldn't do that if I were you." That is correct; they are not you!

The dynamics of siblings can be very complex; however, it is very important that you are able to separate yourself emotionally and mentally from them so you do not become enmeshed, to the point you don't quite know where you start or finish!

I have encountered people who have come from both large and small families, yet regardless of the size, have felt under the shadow of their brothers or sisters, even in adulthood. This usually happens when the younger siblings are allowed to thrive without hindrance (it's called "doing whatever the hell they please") and the older one trails silently (and oftentimes resentfully) in the background

Don't Let Them Stop You – It's Personal!

shouldering responsibilities laid on them by mum and/or dad. It's difficult to set boundaries if you haven't been allowed to set any throughout your childhood (I get it), and this can become even more complex when dealing with your siblings. After all, weren't we (as a rule) taught to play nicely? Share our toys and defer to each other? (In other words, "Stop the fighting!") In some cultures (West African), younger siblings are to call their much older siblings "auntie" or "uncle" as a sign of respect.

Of course, it doesn't mean you respect them, but the implication on your decision making can be huge! E.g., their opinion of your prospective spouse (combined with parental approval/disapproval) can affect your life, leaving you feeling disempowered. You may need to seek some external support to reposition yourself within the family structure.

What 3 areas of life do you believe about your relationship with your siblings has impacted you the most?

1.
_____
_____
_____
_____
_____

2.
_____
_____
_____
_____
_____

Don't Let Them Stop You – It's Personal!

3.

_____
_____
_____
_____

DON'T LET THEM STOP YOU!

What 3 promises do you want to make to yourself after reading this chapter? (I promise I won't look!)

1.

_____
_____
_____
_____

2.

_____
_____
_____
_____

Don't Let Them Stop You – It's Personal!

3.

_____

_____

_____

_____

_____

Your children

You only need one (a child that is!) to have your world turned completely upside down! They come with their own personalities, and you become responsible for much of how they turn out (or so, they would have us believe!) I totally understand parental guilt. This comes with having three children and constantly worrying about if you are meeting their needs on an individual level. Yep, confession time. That was me. One thing I know from personal experience that this feeling can very be draining on your soul, to say the least, especially if you feel you are throwing everything at it in terms of good parenting!

In your quest to be a perfect parent, you can end up putting your life on hold forever if you are not careful! It is important to remember that when you are raising children, you have an element of control over the decisions you make, and do not have to be a slave to your children!

When you consider your own upbringing, you may perhaps be able to view your own circumstances from a different perspective as no two people experience their childhood exactly the same way and you will not try to recreate the childhood for your child that you had (if you are smart!) This took me a while to realise that there is no perfect childhood; we all have to go and *grow* through it in different ways.

Don't Let Them Stop You – It's Personal!

On the other side, your child(ren) can be also very manipulative (Okay, okay not yours! Other people's then!) No one can make you feel quite as guilty as your children (if they choose to leverage it!) What sort of things can they make you feel guilty about?

- Giving birth to them (without having enough money!)
- Loving the other children (sometimes not just siblings) more than them
- Over loving/giving (smothering) them
- Not supporting them enough with their life
- Not helping enough with the grandkids
- Getting over involved in their lives
- Giving too much to the grandkids.

Listen; all the points they make and raise are possibly valid; however, as a parent, you can always hold your hands up, humble yourself, (yes; you can!) give your apologies and make amends. For those of you following cultural modelling for parenting, yet living in a different cultural society, I am not saying you need to abandon your culture; however, you might want to reflect on the principles handed down by your forefathers and decide if these principles are still fit for purpose in this time and generation (stop the eye roll please!)

You do not have to feel attached to the parenting experiences you had as a child and replicate them with your own children. Times have changed, and even the good practices that worked then, may not necessarily work now. If you consider the development of children in chronological years, your true impact is during their formative years and the strategies you use in adolescence is totally different to what you use in early years (just in case you didn't know!)

You don't have to micro-manage your children either. You really don't! If you infantilise them, you will actually contribute to stunting their growth and slow their progress down into adulthood.

Don't Let Them Stop You – It's Personal!

This is also a great way to start the journey of getting your power back from them!

Other relatives – If your anything like me, your other relatives can be a combination of siblings, friends, or even parents. I would highlight that this is totally normal; however, based on how often you see them can be just as influential as the rest in your family.

I want to talk a bit about "enmeshment" – Have you heard of this term?

Enmeshment definition:

Enmeshment [3] is a psychological term used to describe a dysfunctional family dynamic where boundaries between individuals are blurred or non-existent. In enmeshed families, members are overly involved in each other's lives, thoughts, and emotions, and there is a lack of differentiation between the self and the family unit. It explores how enmeshment works in the family structure, its effects on individuals, and the family as a whole, and potential ways to address enmeshment.

Enmeshment is a description of a relationship between two or more people in which personal boundaries are permeable and unclear. This often happens on an emotional level in which two people "feel" each other's emotions, or when one person becomes emotionally escalated and the other family member does as well.

A good example of this is when a teenage son gets anxious and depressed and his mother in turn, gets anxious and depressed. She is taking on her son's emotions, and when the son starts to feel happy again, the mother feels happy again.

Now, it is natural for a parent to be upset when they see the child going through difficulties; however, we are not talking about just feeling sorry here, we are talking about allowing the emotions of your loved ones to incapacitate you to the point it feels as if you are personally sharing the same actual experience. You are enmeshed, when as a mother, you are not able to separate your emotional

Don't Let Them Stop You – It's Personal!

experience from that of your son (or daughter), even though you both may state that you have clear personal boundaries with each other.

Enmeshment between a parent and their children will often result in over involvement in each other's lives so that it makes it hard for the children to become developmentally independent and responsible for his or her choices. This can result in the children growing up to be needy of their parents, even when they are fully grown adults and should be able to make sound decisions for themselves.

Enmeshment often starts with well-intentioned behaviour, such as a parent who wants to be close to their children, or siblings who are protective of each other. However, as time goes on, boundaries become less clear, and individuals become more enmeshed. For instance, a parent may rely on their child for emotional support and validation, leading the child to feel responsible for the parent's well-being. Similarly, siblings may feel responsible for each other's happiness, leading to a lack of independence and difficulty developing their own identities.

Enmeshment can have significant negative effects on individuals and the family as a whole. For instance, individuals in enmeshed families may experience a lack of autonomy, difficulty making decisions, and a sense of being overwhelmed by others' emotions. They may also struggle with developing a sense of self and have difficulty expressing their needs and desires. The family as a whole may experience a lack of healthy communication, difficulty with conflict resolution, and the inability to handle change or separation.

To address enmeshment, it is important to establish clear boundaries and promote healthy differentiation between individuals in the family. This can include encouraging open communication, allowing for individual autonomy, and fostering a sense of independence. It is also important to seek professional help if the enmeshment is severe or has caused significant distress.

Don't Let Them Stop You – It's Personal!

Even though this concept may be new to you (perhaps it has been your norm) enmeshment is a dysfunctional family dynamic where boundaries between individuals are blurred or non-existent. It can have negative effects on individuals and the family as a whole, leading to a lack of autonomy, difficulty with communication and conflict resolution, and an inability to handle change or separation. Addressing enmeshment requires the establishment of clear boundaries and promoting healthy differentiation between individuals in the family.

Some possible causes for enmeshment:
The causes of enmeshment can vary. Sometimes, there is an event or series of occurrences in a family's history that necessitates a parent becoming protective in their child's life. This can be chronic or a life-threatening illness, trauma, or significant social problems in school. At this time, the parent steps in to intervene. This action is quite normal, as parents want to alleviate the suffering of their children in any way they can.

However, while this intervention may have been appropriate at the time, some parents get stuck using the same approach in new settings which results in becoming overly involved in the day-to-day interactions of their children. The base of these types of behaviours is fear that our children cannot build their own resilience. Sometimes, it is based on the fear of our own past experiences being repeated in their lives.

What does it look like?
- A lack of privacy between parents and children as they grow older
- Parents expecting children to be their best friends and always confiding in them
- Children receiving praise for maintaining the family's status quo
- Parents being overly involved in the child's life as they grow up.

Don't Let Them Stop You – It's Personal!

This is NOT the same as being close to your family members. The test is: can you make your own decisions without other family members being upset, even when it has nothing to do with them and will not cause a detrimental effect on them?

What 3 areas of life do you believe about your relationship with your child/children has impacted you the most?

1.
_____
_____
_____
_____
_____

2.
_____
_____
_____
_____
_____

3.
_____
_____
_____
_____
_____

Don't Let Them Stop You – It's Personal!

DON'T LET THEM STOP YOU!

What 3 promises do you want to make to yourself after reading this chapter? (I promise I won't look!)

1.
_____
_____
_____
_____

2.
_____
_____
_____
_____

3.
_____
_____
_____
_____

CHAPTER 3

Friends; Simply the Best?

What do you think of your friends? Are they lovely? Are they supportive, or are they difficult? Spiteful? Sarcastic? (One would argue that the last 3 questions should make you ponder if they are actually friends). We all have an assortment of friends and can loosely put them into the following categories:

- Best Friends
- Close Friends
- Casual Friends
- Frenemies!

We all have friends of varying degrees and connections at different junctures in our lives. It's normal to have friends who are not your family members, and I am very aware that people (especially when they have been hurt) decide they don't want to keep friends! Do you remember when your parents would check and monitor your friends? It's funny how some of them can see in others what we couldn't see at the time. Some outspoken parents would blatantly say "I don't like him or her" or "Just be careful with that one," and some would interrogate you and want to know more about this "friend".

I admit this may be more of a cultural response to our children having friends. It's like an antenna went up and they somehow know that particular individuals wouldn't be good for us! My parents were really good at this, and I now understand it wasn't an amazing gift, but they had good observation skills!

As we grow into adulthood; however, we no longer have the long arm of parental guidance watching over us; instead, we choose our own friends (well, I certainly hope so!)

Don't Let Them Stop You – It's Personal!

The challenge is not keeping friends, the challenge is sometimes not knowing how to navigate friendships in a healthy way that brings mutual benefit. Don't get me wrong, friendships can at times be delicate, even difficult to manage, but it has to be worth the effort and not a full-on emotional drain of your time!

The deeper question to ask yourself is: What does a healthy friendship [4] look like?

Before we dive deeper into that question, let's do a health check with your current friendships. It's good to evaluate your friends (not to criticise) in order to understand if there is positive value to spending your time with them; whether in person or on the phone.

When you are with your friend(s), how do you feel? Happy? Relaxed? Awkward? Uncomfortable? Anxious to impress?

What is your position in your circle of friends? (if you move with a group) – Just in case you didn't know, someone is the head of that group! Where do you fit in?

What are the benefits of having these friends? There needs to be some benefits, whether they are good listeners, or they make you laugh, or even if they cause you to look at life from different angles. Why did you choose this person or people as your friends, or did they choose you? – What was it about them that attracted you to forming a friendship with them?

Are you able to recognise when your friendships have reached their expiry date without it happening as a result of a big drama? (like a reality TV show!)

Are you friends with individuals who have narcissism traits and in turn, make you feel insecure or unsure of your own identity?

Do your friends consume all your time and energy?

One of my favourite movies is *"Never been kissed."* Firstly, because I am a romantic person and love a movie which has a happy ending!

Don't Let Them Stop You – It's Personal!

Secondly, I believe this is a powerful story about friendships and how they work in particular settings.

Without giving the storyline away, I learned 3 things from this film:

1. As you get older, you need to know the positions in friendship groups.
2. You sometimes need the help of someone else to open the eyes of others – evaluation of friendships is important and to understand where you fit in with your friends.
3. Friendships are great; however, as you progress in life, it is important to recognise when it's time to change your circle (or at least adjust it!)

Now the filmmakers may not have had this in mind when they were creating the story, so this is my personal interpretation – either way, if you are into romcoms, it's worth the watch!

Let's go over the 3 points in more detail…

Getting older – It's true folks, as you grow older, you have less friends; not more. Don't worry about that. It's a good thing (in my opinion). It means there is less stretching of one's time and quality of friendship becomes the name of the game. You can ask yourself thought-provoking questions such as: What is my position in this friendship? Am I bringing anything to the relationship or, is the other person bringing anything to the relationship? Does it matter? I hear you ask! Yes, because time is a precious commodity, and as we get older, we don't have as much time!

Remember this is about not letting "them" stop you! You have a right to not feel guilty about assessing who is in your life and if they should have a place there! Because life is complicated (and so are people!), it can be difficult to see the wood from the trees when trying to work out what friendships are valid and those that are not.

So here are a few pointers:

Don't Let Them Stop You – It's Personal!

Behaviours – I am sure you have heard of the saying: "Actions speaks louder than words?" I don't know who came up with it, but it is a powerful statement and very true! How do your friend(s) treat you? Do you feel like an after-thought? Do they make you feel paranoid or self-conscious? Do you feel they only call you when they need something, or want to offload? Do they make you feel comfortable and valued? Do they consider your personal circumstances? E.g., are they considerate of the fact you have children to look after, or a demanding job, or a household to run?

HOW DO THEY MAKE YOU FEEL?

If conversations always leave you feeling drained, just double check you are not being used as an emotional buffer. When you are full up mentally or emotionally of other people's "stuff," as great as a distraction this can be, you need to stay mindful that their emotional dramas are not slowing you down!

I love the Proverb "Stop drinking bush for other people's fever." In other words, don't take on other people's problems which are invariably nothing to do with you! What does it look like? Getting angry on behalf of your friend, getting caught up in the fight, feeling aggrieved and upset based on what they shared with you. All of these emotions and you are not directly involved! Don't let people target you for their emotional use (it's quite a narcissistic trait actually). A quick way to analyse this type of friendship is to start sharing your "problems" and see if they are still interested, or find an excuse to attend to something or someone else!

I like to remind people that although friendships will involve components of being supportive, you cannot "help" everyone and you cannot "save" everyone. If this is the major components of your friendship, then I would safely conclude that this is more of a mentoring/counsellor relationship than one of mutual benefit and admiration of each other.

My advice to you?

Don't Let Them Stop You – It's Personal!

STOP TAKING PILLS FOR OTHER PEOPLE'S HEADACHES!

Trust – Can you trust your friend with your visions and dreams? When you speak about yourself, are you showered with encouragement and left feeling inspired? After spending time with them, does the experience leave you with a desire to improve or reach for your goals? Do you feel you can have a private conversation with them and it will stay that way? If you are facing struggles, can you share with them without fear of judgement? Can you be 100% yourself?

Having said all of that, you should be mindful about what you disclose with friends, (and dare I say different friends earn different levels of disclosure) under the description of being "transparent."

YOU SHOULD NEVER FEEL OBLIGATED TO SHARE YOUR PERSONAL INFORMATION OR EXPERIENCES; NEITHER SHOULD YOU TOLERATE PRESSURE TO DO SO!

Progressing through life – Did you know that a bit like literal death, friendships also die a death? Very few of us have not experienced some type of loss, and the end of a friendship can feel like a loss (even if we are relieved!) Welcome to life's journey where our lives are enhanced by changing, amending, or repositioning our friendships. Sometimes, we want to hang on to relationships which have expired (don't worry you are perfectly normal), and we need to examine why this is.

Could it be that you feel you have given so much of your personal information that you feel uneasy to let them go? Have you become co-dependent* on them over time without realising it? *Co-dependent No more* by Melodie Beattie, is a great book to describe this type of relationship. You may be a victim of a toxic relationship and not recognise it yet (or maybe you do now you are reading this

Don't Let Them Stop You – It's Personal!

book), and yet the signs and red flags are all around you, but there remains a blind spot or a fear of the unknown.

Can you recover from leaving a toxic friendship? Absolutely! Will you lose some more friends as a result? Highly probable! Will it take some courage? Absolutely! You will have to face your fears (and your attachment issues) in order to make the progress necessary to move forward. Remember, there are nearly 8 billion people on the planet…you can always find new friends who are compatible with your values and principles, and most importantly, to have people in your life who want to be friends with you, not based on what you may or may not have in terms of possessions, but rather your contribution on a compassionate and caring level.

The most difficult relationships to extricate yourself from is not always family; it can be the "friend zone." Some will die a natural death and others may linger on the life support machine. Some can be revived and take on a new dynamic, and others will have to be given a dignified funeral! I will not minimise how painful this can be; however, we must sometimes endure a little suffering to be free (just ask my ancestors!)

Look, the reality is – it will be impossible to navigate life without changing circles (that's if you want to get on, of course, and obviously you do, otherwise why read this book?). It is possible to manage the dynamics of one-to-one friendships or friendship circles if you have more than one group of friends. Many years ago, somebody once said (I can't remember who it was,) that "peer pressure doesn't stop when you leave high school; it stops when you are dead!" Peer pressure, although not discussed as adults remains a dynamic that needs to be handled with skill and wisdom. Sad, but true!

YOU MAY HAVE TO PROMOTE, DEMOTE OR REMOVE FRIENDS FROM YOUR LIFE. THIS IS PERFECTLY NORMAL AND ACCEPTABLE BASED ON WHERE YOU ARE IN YOUR LIFE'S JOURNEY.

Don't Let Them Stop You – It's Personal!

At any level of encounter, we can be in awe of our friends and acquaintances, especially when we *feel* they are more "successful" than we are or "stronger" than we are or "cleverer" than we are. The wake-up call for you (if you believe any of that stuff,) is that *no one* really is better than us, or has a truly better life. Yes, it's true they may have more money than you, they may have the job you always wanted to have and maybe the ideal partner you wished you could have. Let me console that a lot of what we see is not the sum total of someone's life; it's just a snapshot!

Oftentimes, we do not have insight into how people live their daily lives (unless we are living with them) and in the social media age, we have all become very good at showing off the "good" bits and hiding the not-so-good bits. Some people can do this in person as well, and it's all designed to make people feel jealous! I know! Hard to believe, isn't it?

I recall the story of a woman who constantly bombarded her work colleagues with stories of her lovely husband and how much he did for her. She even wore to work the fur coat that he bought her, making her the envy of her friends. The only problem was none of it was true! She went out of her way to 'taunt' her friends with her amazing relationship, only for them to discover that it was not true, and in fact, her husband had actually left her for someone else!

The question you can ask yourself is to what extent are my friendships impacting or influencing my life decisions? Another question is are you taking your accountability of them too far? It is a mistake to believe that we are not more easily influenced than anyone else. If we are human, we are subject to all kinds to subtle and overt influences of our friends.

You may have heard about social influence? No? Okay, let me explain: Psychologists have spent decades studying the power of social influence, and the way in which it manipulates people's opinions and behaviours. Specifically, social influence refers to the way in which individuals change their ideas and actions to meet the demands of a social group, perceived authority, social role or a minority within a group wielding influence over the majority.

Don't Let Them Stop You – It's Personal!

Most of us encounter social influence in many forms on a regular basis. For example, a student may alter his or her behaviour to match that of other students in a class. The majority-held opinions of a group of friends are likely to inform the views of new members to that social group. Furthermore, we are influenced by the requests of people who are seen as holding positions of authority. For instance, an employee will follow the orders of his supervisors in order to please them.

Why people accept social influence

There are a number of reasons why people allow social influences to affect their thoughts and behaviours. One reason is that we often conform to the norms of a group to gain acceptance of its members. Supporters of a football team voluntarily wear shirts of their teams to feel a part of the group. Friends may also wear similar clothing to their peers to experience a sense of belonging and to emphasise their shared ideas.

An example of this is:

A person may feel pressurised to smoke because the rest of their friends are. Normative social influence tends to lead to compliance because the person smokes just for show, but deep down, they wish not to smoke. This means any change of behaviour is temporary. A healthy friendship is one where your friends accept your decision-making unconditionally, without trying to sway you, put you off your choices, or challenging you outright because they wouldn't do it!

FINALLY...

Your good friends will not stop speaking to you or exclude you because they don't approve of your life choices (unless it's something illegal or very dangerous). If you find yourself conforming because you don't want to feel rejected or abandoned, you need to revisit that friendship and ask yourself is it worth losing a piece of you to keep the relationship going?

Don't Let Them Stop You – It's Personal!

Three questions to ask yourself:

1. Who is having the biggest impact in your life now from your circle of friends?

_____
_____
_____
_____
_____

2. Who is has had the greatest impact in your life in the past from my friends?

_____
_____
_____
_____
_____

3. Is there anything I feel I need to change or do differently in managing my circle?

_____
_____
_____
_____
_____

Don't Let Them Stop You – It's Personal!

DON'T LET THEM STOP YOU!

What 3 promises do you want to make to yourself after reading this chapter? (I promise I won't look!)

1.
_____
_____
_____
_____

2.
_____
_____
_____
_____

3.
_____
_____
_____
_____

CHAPTER 4

Significant Others – What's Love Got To Do With It?

It's great when it works; not so great when it doesn't! I am not a relationship coach; I am a business coach; however, I do understand relationships and what good ones look like…I recognise that as much as you may feel love for your significant other, you might also have some other feelings which make you feel a bit "less than."

Being in a loving relationship is the fundamental right of every human being (if that's what they want), and as we unpick who may be in your life and what they contribute, we cannot bypass our nearest and dearest!

Cultures may play a key part of how relationships work within marriage, co-habiting (or whatever it's called where you come from).

In some cultures, the male takes a clear dominant role, and the female whilst being able to make some decisions, must defer to the preference of her husband. In other words, he has the final say.

I am not here to step on or challenge other cultures and their practices (I actually celebrate the differences we have as individuals, and in my opinion, it is important to acknowledge and respect the culture of others); they are what they are. At the same time, there are some commonalities when it comes to what love feels like and what it may look like externally.

For the purposes of this book, I am going to take a "western" view of things. What does this mean? This means that I am going to work on the assumption, but within personal relationships, each individual is able to make choices based on what meets their needs and how their needs are met as considering the needs of their life partner.

Don't Let Them Stop You – It's Personal!

In these constantly changing times, it can be hard to keep up with all the new rules that are continually being created by which we must set the benchmark of what a good relationship looks like.

The bigger question is, is your current relationship a help or a hindrance to your progress? When wanting to progress or make progressive decisions for your life, do you come up against a wall of opposition? Are you made to feel guilty? Do you feel that if your partner is not included, you cannot proceed?

So, what place has love in all of this you may ask? Does anybody marry to fight with their spouse? Does anybody make decisions to deliberately upset their spouse? If the answer is yes, then you have a different kind of problem which cannot be addressed in this book!

This is a difficult chapter, because it is here where one will dig deeper into exploring what your needs are and how they can be met. The book is titled: 'Don't let them stop you!' So, how do we navigate them if it's a spouse?

I have come across friends and acquaintances in my lifetime, come up against this problem, and can I say here that this is not always about women feeling oppressed or suffocated, but also about men who have felt oppressed and suffocated, both emotionally and mentally. As a result, neither party have been able to move into their full potential on an individual level. Personally, it is heart-rending to see such situations.

I will say at this point, that in my opinion, nine times out of 10, there isn't a deliberate attempt to sabotage anyone's future; however, it can be a collision of worlds when two parties who were united in vision are now sitting on the opposing sides of the fence, and the visions they once shared, are no longer relevant to one or the other. This was a contributing factor in my own relationship.

Sometimes, goals are no longer the same. Is there anything wrong with that? All I would say at this point is it can be extremely difficult! It *is* possible for couples to outgrow their relationship; it's also possible for couples to stay together and recognise they are on divergent paths and embrace the new normal of their relationships. The success rate of this being managed well however, would largely depend on how flexible each party is in their thinking, how comfortable they are with the other person not changing, and lastly, not being threatened by any significant changes.

Now I realise at this point, some might argue that surely, love includes making sacrifices. I agree with that 100%; however, we need to look at what sacrifice looks like, the challenges within that sacrifice, and if there are any negotiables.

So, what's love got to do with it?

Within the boundaries of a healthy relationship, couples will love and care for each other. Normally, in a relationship, is still in the early stages, and a healthy couple at least likes each other (in a way that's more than just physical attraction; after all, looks will fade over time!). Healthy relationships are built on more than just physical intimacy, looks and other trivial things. I am sure you have heard this before; however, let me remind you that having a solid personal relationship takes work and the ability to build a real connection between you and your spouse. Is it easy? No! Is it worth it? It needs to be!

Some initial questions for you:

- Do I love my spouse? - People *do* fall out of love with each other!
- Would I still want to be with them if they were poor or sick? – If the answer is "no" – then you have reviewed your position!
- Is there a deep connection between us? Have you found a soulmate? (Notice I said "a" soulmate, as I believe with 8 billion people on the planet, you can have more than one in your lifetime. This of course is purely my personal opinion!)

Don't Let Them Stop You – It's Personal!

If you feel like the love is fading in your relationship, it might be a warning sign that all is not well (and a weekend away won't necessarily fix it either). When this happens, it's important to address it to see if these feelings are temporary or not. I would suggest that you seek counselling. You also need to consider your mental health and well-being whilst you are addressing any issues.

These issues can be very complex; however, if you are involved in any of the following:

- A co-dependent relationship
- A parental-style relationship
- A coercive control relationship
- A narcissistic relationship.

Those mentioned above are most likely to be the relationships which will hinder your personal development and progress, and ultimately stop you from reaching your desired goals (and that goal may just be having some peace of mind!).

I could have gone in a different direction with personal relationships; however, when considering the title of this book, I would be doing an injustice if I didn't address these types of relationships. Before launching into this section, I will encourage you to seek external support if you are identifying with being in one of these relationships and you are feeling unhappy about it.

THE CODEPENDENT RELATIONSHIP

What is a co-dependent relationship?

In a co-dependent relationship [5], there tends to be a severe imbalance of power. Often, one person may be giving much more time, energy and focus to the other person, who consciously or unconsciously takes advantage of the situation in order to maximize their needs and desires. The interesting thing is you can have a co-

Don't Let Them Stop You – It's Personal!

dependent relationship with *anyone* including your boss, friends, colleagues, or family members.

The challenge is that it may take a while for you to realise that you are in this type of relationship. It can feel mutually beneficial at first, and then you suddenly realise the other person's needs and desires take precedent over yours (or vice versa). Don't get me wrong, it's lovely if you can be supportive, especially if it gives you a positive feeling in knowing you're contributing to someone else's success and happiness. However, if this is happening at the loss of your own values, responsibilities and needs, you can end up losing sight of who you are!

Even if you start of on a high note because you love to "help" the person you love, always remember that you cannot save anyone! (No, honestly you can't!). You just end up feeling resentful and being called a control freak!

What are the signs of a co-dependent relationship?

A common theme is they usually involve some form of self-sacrifice and/or neglect.

You feel like you need to save the person from themselves

In a co-dependent relationship, one person often takes on the role of a caretaker: As the caretaker, you (not saying you, specifically, but it could be you), step into repair, mend, improve, come up with solutions or spending your time picking up the pieces of the errors they have made. It sounds exhausting and it is! In the early days, you believe the behaviour is redeemable (why shouldn't it be? Nobody's perfect, right?) however, you can end up forgetting that it is the responsibility of the other person to make real and lasting change. You forget that you are limited in what you can do. Result? A one-sided relationship.

Don't Let Them Stop You – It's Personal!

You have a desire to change who *they* are

Remember the song with the words by songwriter Billy Joel "I love you just the way you are?" Hmmm, sounds perfect and romantic! What's the first line again? Something about not changing to make me happy! Let me explain that as humans, there is sometimes an innate desire to turn our spouses into our "product." We need to stop doing that! Don't get me wrong, giving a hand with someone who wants to improve themselves is fine, but wanting to change someone's fundamental difference in character and beliefs is a totally different matter. Want some examples?

- You are fairly introverted and like to spend time in quiet places, but your partner is a party animal.
- You like staying indoors or hosting intimate dinners and hope to convert them to your lifestyle.
- You make yourself go out when you don't enjoy those types of environments in the hopes that your small act of kindness (sacrifice) could persuade them to give up a life of partying.

Be very careful; you may be practicing co-dependent behaviours!

You feel selfish looking after yourself (AKA self-care)

If you are becoming a slave to your partner's needs to the point where you feel guilty doing things from which they will not benefit (e.g., your favourite pastimes or hobbies) or you feel they have to constantly be present at whatever you are doing, this is a sign you may be co-dependent.

How did you spend your time before you met them? Do you no longer engage in the things you used to do because you don't want to, or because your partner's needs are now taking priority over yours?

Don't get me wrong, some people love to spend all their time together, especially if they are aging or there is some illness

Don't Let Them Stop You – It's Personal!

involved. Even so, this should always be by mutual consent and not because one person feels bad to go off anywhere without the other.

You struggle to articulate how you feel about your relationship

If someone asks about you and your partner (taking boundaries into consideration of course, see previous chapters!), how do you respond? How does the question make you feel? Do you need to take a moment before you answer?

Are you so focused on your partner and their needs that you are not really take the time to process your own feelings and emotions? If this has become a habit, then this can result in avoidance of your own problems or feelings and substituting them with a kind of "high" that comes from meeting your partner's needs or rescuing them from their problems. It's nice, but is it helpful for you?

The challenge is that when you are operating in co-dependency, you can't see what you are in and don't notice that in focusing on someone else, you may not even think that you have needs to be met!

You feel anxious when you don't hear from them

I am not talking about when you have arranged to meet them, and they don't show up, or if they agreed to contact you and are normally very reliable in their communication.

I am talking about getting stressed out over whether or not your partner has read their phone message. Are you constantly checking your phone to see if they have called you, even if there is no reason why they should? Do you create disasters in your mind about what could happen to them just because you are not physically in the same space as them or one of you is away on a trip? Are you borderline obsessed with the need to know where they are every moment of the day? (For no justifiable reason?) It is possible that your partner has

Don't Let Them Stop You – It's Personal!

become your comfort blanket and you have become a needy individual!

You have trouble being alone

Do you struggle being on your own, with your own thoughts? Is all your time spent with your partner and meeting their needs (at their requests or yours?)

Are you uncomfortable with spending quiet time with nothing to do for your partner? Could it be that it feels easier to put your time and attention into your partner and not address issues that make you unhappy or could improve your current situation?

You often make plans, then cancel them to spend time with your partner

Believe it or not, this action is closely linked to self-care! Why? If your relationship is taking a shape which means you are spending less time with your other loved ones and friends, not out of true choice, but out of the fear of being away from your partner, this is an alarm bell and a sign you could be enmeshed! (Also see previous chapters.)

Your living space looks more like theirs than yours

Have you reorganised your home to make it look more like what your partner wishes to have, than what makes you feel comfortable? This can naturally be a bit challenging when you have opposing tastes in décor, home furnishings and colours. The point is your home needs to feel like a familiar space even if your partner is not there for a while, because it's all of what they like, and very little of your personal preferences. You may have to go on a quest to reclaim some of your taste and what your home should look like for you!

Don't Let Them Stop You – It's Personal!

You are being made to feel that you are too demanding

Are you finding that you are becoming quieter and not voicing your opinions like you used to? Are you afraid of what the results will be if you speak up? Does your partner tell you (or make you feel) that you are too demanding no matter how small the request? Do you find that when you try to resolve a situation, you get a blank or negative response? Are you left feeling guilty for raising specific issues which bother or concern you, or second guessing yourself and your feelings? Look out! Your partner may be gaslighting you!

Back to the "B" word "Boundaries." You will know when things are going wrong if their behaviour escalates in a negative fashion when you attempt to press the reset button on the relationship and establish healthy boundaries!

If you try to resolve some issues by setting up healthy boundaries and your partner's behaviour grows worse in spite of your efforts, this is a definite sign that from their standpoint, their own needs take priority over your own needs. Unfortunately, these types of behaviours can lead to deep feelings of resentment or regret, creating an unending cycle of distress for both people.

DON'T LET THEM STOP YOU!

Is there anything you have just read that reminds you of your current relationship?

_____

_____

_____

_____

Don't Let Them Stop You – It's Personal!

What 3 promises do you want to make to yourself after reading this chapter? (I promise I won't look!)

1.

2.

3.

Don't Let Them Stop You – It's Personal!

THE PARENT-CHILD STYLE RELATIONSHIP

As adults, the assumption is that when entering into a relationship, it is highly likely that you will relate to each other as equals. This is not always the case and may take a little time to discover that one partner takes on the majority of the responsibility. When this happens, a parent-child relationship dynamic can develop. Should this not be addressed over time, you can find that you are left feeling frustrated and dissatisfied and impact your emotional well-being.

To be able to understand the parent-child relationship dynamic, you need to have an idea of what it looks like from an everyday perspective.

Some behaviours are more obvious than others, but in real terms, they show a lack of respect (you may not be doing this deliberately, but it is what it is!) for your partner as an adult, and for your equality in the relationship:

- Waking your partner up in the morning
- When traveling, you pack your partner's suitcase
- You are overprotective
- You are the official reminder person—whether it is to take medications, finish a task, or be on time somewhere
- You believe one of your roles is to correct your partner's behaviour
- You buy your partner's clothes
- You fill out medical or legal forms for your partner
- You keep track of your partner's belongings like eyeglasses, car keys, or wallet
- You make appointments with doctors for your partner
- You often cater to your partner's every need
- You pick out what clothes you think your partner should wear
- You pick up after your partner
- You style your partner's hair

Don't Let Them Stop You – It's Personal!

- You think nothing of putting food on your partner's plate, cutting up their meat, or pestering them to eat all the vegetables on their plate
- Your conversation style with your partner uses "baby talk" or a parental tone of voice.

The good news is that you can break this pattern and establish a more equal partnership!

The parent-child relationship dynamic takes place when one party in the romantic relationship takes (consciously or subconsciously), on the role of the parent, and their partner takes on the role of the child.

Why does this dynamic even exist? There could be several reasons why this behaviour arises. The main point is the power dynamic of the relationship is unequal. The challenge is that this can lead to resentment and discontentment. If you take a moment to think about it; a parent takes charge and makes the rules. This also is a type of co-dependency which may work until the "child" in the relationship decides they have had enough, or the "parent" becomes resentful of their role.

An example of this is as follows: one person can take on the role of the parent and the other person, the child, when it comes to finances and the roles can reverse with domestic tasks. Both the "parent" and the "child" can end up resenting each other for being too bossy, or not helping out enough. This can lead to a breakdown in communication and intimacy. In this dynamic, the "parent" will ask the "child" to complete a task and follow up to see if it was done. The "child" often will not complete the task on purpose, and the dynamic continues.

What does the parent-partner role look like?

Who defines each role? Those who are given to nurturing and rescuing others are more inclined to take on the "parent" role. For them, there is a joy that comes from looking after others, and it is often the way that they show love. The challenge is they tend to be controlling and want things done their way! However, they can also believe their way is the only right way to complete a task! They can also be quite demanding, become punitive and feel that they are superior to their partner.

They take the view their partner has as someone that needs to be taken care of because they are irresponsible, helpless, or incompetent (and can I say that this can be because the person presents themselves as such!). Their difficulty is they have a hard time respecting their partner's boundaries or to even trust them to do the right thing. The unhealthy results can lead to the "parent" having a more anxious attachment style and feel uncomfortable confronting irresponsible behaviour and setting appropriate boundaries. Eventually, they can build up resentment toward their partner accusing them of not contributing as much to the relationship as they are!

What does the child-partner role look like?

The partner that takes on the "child" role will usually take a more passive role. Initially, they might even enjoy the concept of being taken care of by someone. Interests and hobbies outside of the partnership can take up a lot of their time and attention. They can end up feeling disrespected by their partner leading to withdrawal from the relationship.

Because they are in the "child" role, they can find it difficult to establish firm boundaries and may resort to passive-aggressive behaviours to get their way. It is likely that the partner in the "child" role could have a more avoidant attachment style which can be inclined to withdraw from any signs of conflict and their partner. They could feel victimised by their partner, but at the same time, come to depend on them. They can also feel somewhat helpless in the relationship.

Don't Let Them Stop You – It's Personal!

The "child" partner can end up resenting the "parent" partner feeling that they cross boundaries in terms of involvement, as well as resenting unwarranted advice. The response? To act out their feeling of resentments either overtly or covertly.

How does this attraction work?

At the beginning of the relationship, the parent-child dynamic can be comforting. For the "child" partner, it can feel emotionally flattering to be get so much attention. While for the "parent" partner, they are able to nurture someone who seems to value them. It is possible that both partners have seen, first hand, this type of interaction in their family, so to them, this dynamic is a normal way of relating. The partner that takes on the child role can feel cared for, while the one that takes on the parent role feels needed. Parent partners need to control their environment and happily spend a lot of energy on their relationship, and "child" partners can focus on whatever their interests may be outside of the relationship. Overtime, problems develop as the inequality in this dynamic becomes more obvious and leads to resentment from both partners.

Is it possible to change the dynamics?

We are talking about dynamics here, not trying to change the person! Aside from the fact that some couples are happy with the status, the parent-child dynamic in relationships are usually toxic and can erode effective communication and intimacy. What if you believe that your relationship fits this pattern, it is essential to change the dynamic and create a more equitable-based relationship. It means that both partners should equally contribute to the relationship and make joint decisions. Both the "parent" partner and the "child" partner will need to try to be more open in their communications and work to establish effective boundaries to break the pattern. The "parent" partner will need to give up some of their control and depend more on their partner for support. On the other hand, the "child" partner will need to increase their efforts to take on more responsibility and contribute more to the relationship overall.

Don't Let Them Stop You – It's Personal!

What can the person in the parent-partner role do?

If this is you, you will need to let your spouse contribute in their own way that is comfortable for them. Stop being so controlling! You may initially feel anxious about whether things will get done, or that everything is falling apart, but if you are going to build any trust in your partner, this approach will be essential. How? You need to back off and allow your partner to do things their way, even if you feel the outcome doesn't meet your standards. Ask your partner for their opinions and give them a sense that they also have some control. You could make a list of tasks that needs to be done and make a joint decision about who will do what. If you are more open about your needs, this can help keep resentment from building and increase your emotional intimacy, and being more vulnerable with your partner can actually deepen your connection. You don't have to be a super-human!

What can the person in the child-partner role do?

If you identify as this individual, then you will need to make a concerted effort and take on a more active role in the relationship. It will be up to you to set firm boundaries around the way you expect to be treated (don't ask your "parent" partner, okay?) If you experience your partner talking down to you or rebuking you, you need to let them know (or remind them) that it is not okay. Take an adult approach and agree to tasks that you can complete and follow through. Do this instead of engaging in passive-aggressive behaviours, because you do not feel you are getting your own way! It is possible for you to be direct. How? By letting your partner know that the relationship is important, and you are there for them. Be supportive to your partner when they are struggling with something, and take the time to listen to them. The key is to come together as a team and make joint decisions about your relationship and how your home is run.

Don't rule out couple counselling if you cannot turn around the parent-child dynamic in your relationship. This course of action can be constructive in helping you recognise the pattern and understand

Don't Let Them Stop You – It's Personal!

where this is coming from. If you are willing and have the courage, you can take steps to create a more equal partnership. This can also help to improve your intimacy and overall relationship satisfaction.

Is there anything you have just read that reminds you of your current relationship?

_____
_____
_____
_____
_____

What 3 promises do you want to make to yourself after reading this chapter? (I promise I won't look!)

1.
_____
_____
_____
_____
_____

2.
_____
_____

Don't Let Them Stop You – It's Personal!

_____

_____

_____

3.

_____

_____

_____

_____

THE COERCIVE CONTROL RELATIONSHIP

There is much said in these current times about coercive control [6] within relationships, and this act is now a criminal offence. It is good to remember that most abusive relationships rarely start out this way (otherwise you would run off at the very beginning!). Coercive control can be difficult to detect due to it normally being a slow deliberate process that develops over time.

The challenge is by the time you realise something isn't quite right, it can be difficult to leave the relationship straight away due to your emotional involvement.

It is important that you know the signs. These can include the following:

- **Being critical and using verbal abuse**: shouting, mocking, name-calling, putting you down.

- **Putting pressure on you**: sulking; threatening to withhold money, disconnecting the phone and internet, taking away or

Don't Let Them Stop You – It's Personal!

destroying your mobile, tablet or laptop, taking the car away, taking the children away; threatening to report you to the police, social services or the mental health team unless you comply with their demands; threatening or attempting self-harm and suicide; withholding or pressuring you to use drugs or other substances; lying to your friends and family about you; telling you that you have no choice in any decisions.

- **Being disrespectful to you**: persistently putting you down in front of other people, not listening or responding when you talk; interrupting your telephone calls; taking money from your purse without asking; refusing to help with childcare or housework.

- **Isolating you from others**: monitoring or blocking your phone calls, e-mails and social media accounts, preventing you from seeing friends and relatives; shutting you in the house.

- **Harassing you**: following you; checking up on you; not allowing you any privacy, accompanying you everywhere you go.

- **Breaking your trust**: lying to you; withholding information from you; being jealous; having other relationships; breaking promises and shared agreements.

- **Using sexual violence**: using force, threats or intimidation to make you perform sexual acts; having sex with you when you don't want it; forcing you to look at pornographic material; constant pressure and harassment into having sex when you don't want to, forcing you to have sex with other people; also, any degrading treatment related to your sexuality.

- **Making threats to you**: making angry gestures; using physical size to intimidate; shouting you down; destroying

Don't Let Them Stop You – It's Personal!

your possessions; breaking things; punching walls; wielding a weapon.

- **Using physical violence against you**: punching; slapping; hitting; biting; pinching; kicking; pulling your hair out; pushing; shoving; burning; strangling, pinning you down, holding you by the neck, restraining you.

- **Denial**: saying the abuse doesn't happen; saying you caused the abuse; begging for forgiveness; saying it will never happen again; saying they can't control their anger; being publicly gentle and patient.

- **Using coercive control to harm, punish, or frighten you**: depriving you of basic needs, such as food; monitoring your time / your activity throughout the day i.e. use of hidden cameras; denying you freedom; taking control over aspects of your everyday life, such as where you can go, who you can see, what you can wear and when you can sleep; depriving you access to support services, such as medical services; repeatedly putting you down; humiliating, degrading or dehumanising you; controlling your finances / limiting your access to money).

The first important step is acknowledging these factors in order to prevent and stop the abuse. If you are experiencing abusive behaviour, it is important to remember that the abuse is not your fault, that domestic abuse is against the law, and you don't have to deal with this on your own because there is a lot of support available.

DON'T LET THEM STOP YOU!

Is there anything you have just read that reminds you of your current relationship?

Don't Let Them Stop You – It's Personal!

_____
_____
_____

What 3 promises do you want to make to yourself after reading this chapter? (I promise I won't look!)

1.
_____
_____
_____
_____

2.
_____
_____
_____
_____

3.
_____
_____

Don't Let Them Stop You – It's Personal!

THE NARCISSITIC RELATIONSHIP

If you are in a relationship with someone who has narcissistic traits [7], you may find yourself feeling isolated and unloved. You can be worn down emotionally and your self-esteem impacted due to repeated criticisms, gaslighting, and negative reactions to the mildest of offences. Narcissism has a spectrum between grandiose and being vulnerable. Their core need is to feel special all the time and they have a propensity to break the following rules:

1. They present themselves as very charming

When you first met, they seemed like the perfect partner. They were sociable, kind, generous, and very affectionate. They go out of their way to show you how they feel with big displays of affection. They appear to be very interested in your wellbeing and show they care about you, treating you like a prince or princess. Another term for this is called "love bombing." They keep this up until you start to trust their intentions are pure and you believe you are soul mates. However, over the process of time, their attitude slowly changes, and they begin to devalue you (you are not the prince or princess anymore!) and this begins the cycle of narcissistic abuse, followed by their need to keep you in their life. You become a source of supply to them.

2. Conversations are always about them

If you listen carefully, you will find that the conversation is always about them, even if you start off with making it about something else! They will find a way to bring it back to themselves. The topic

Don't Let Them Stop You – It's Personal!

of conversation is always redirected towards their life and experiences, and the narcissist will also accuse you of being insecure. It could be about an incident in their past or some accomplishment of theirs. They will often interrupt a story about you in order to bring the attention back to themselves. If your opinion differs from theirs, they might correct you, dismiss you, or simply ignore you.

3. They expect preferential treatment

They feel entitled to special privileges. They feel their very presence means they should be put first in everything e.g., everyone is waiting for them at a restaurant, they don't want to wait their turn in a queue and will hustle themselves to the front of a line. When they don't get what they want, they behave like a child either having a tantrum or by sulking (it's embarrassing to watch). They struggle to put anyone else's needs before their own.

4. They act like they are more important than others

There is an old-fashioned phrase used to describe someone who thinks they are great and above everyone else. This term is known as having "Delusions of Grandeur." It is used to describe someone who fancies themselves and are not justified in doing so. They will happily show off about their accomplishments or skills, wealth etc., (which are usually greatly exaggerated!), while ignoring or minimising what others may have achieved. They appear to be convinced of their own superiority, when in reality, none of us are greater than anyone else!

5. They need compliments like you need air to breathe!

Nothing wrong with getting a nice compliment every now and then; however, narcissists use this external validation as a type of fuel. They use compliments to boost their ego which in turn, reinforces their sense of feeling superior. If they are constantly looking for compliments from you or from others when you are out in public, and they are relying on that, it's likely that the narcissist is looking for supply. The expression "a little praise goes a long way" does not apply to them!

6. They lack empathy and disregard your feelings

Because they are preoccupied with their own feelings and needs, narcissists seem cold and detached when you need emotional support. Making a sincere apology is challenging for them, as well as accepting responsibility for any harm they cause. It may go something like: "Oh, sorry about that, but if you (they) hadn't..." So, they are sorry, but not sorry!

7. They focus on things which are superficial

Their put great emphasis on their own appearance, beauty and social status. They happily invest a lot of effort (and money) into their own appearance and have no problem criticising any perceived flaws in other people, including you! They may even expect you to meet their standards of perfection because they see you as an extension of themselves.

8. They don't have many friends (if any)

Should they have any long-time friends, it may be those friends who are empaths and may be utilizing people-pleasing to feel good about themselves. If you find that someone doesn't have friends or they have a hard time making friends, it could be indicative of narcissism.

It's important to note that situations such as friends moving away or being in different life stages doesn't mean that someone is narcissistic. Friendship takes effort from both people, so the qualities that make a friendship work must be reciprocated.

Don't Let Them Stop You – It's Personal!

9. They are nice and charming if they feel it will benefit them

They are capable of superficial charm and appear to be extremely confident (notice that this is all on the surface). Unfortunately, it is more of a performance than coming from the heart. You will note that this engaging social manner will change in a short moment of time, and they become hostile if they feel they are being slighted or dismissed by others. It is what is called a narcissistic injury.

10. They are extremely sensitive to criticism

They respond to constructive criticism (regardless of how well-meaning) with heated arguments or sudden detachment. A common response is to judge, criticise, or gaslight you, blaming you for the problem or offense you brought to their attention. Feedback is not a gift to present to them!

11. They are often trying to manipulate others

They use others to meet their own needs or to fulfil their own dreams. At times, this involves portraying themselves as a victim of unfair circumstances. This is done in an attempt to persuade you or guilt you into doing something that is not in your best interest, but serves their needs.

Is there anything you have just read that reminds you of your current relationship?

_____

_____

_____

_____

_____

Don't Let Them Stop You – It's Personal!

What 3 promises do you want to make to yourself after reading this chapter? (I promise I won't look!)

1.
_____
_____
_____
_____
_____

2.
_____
_____
_____
_____
_____

3.
_____
_____
_____
_____
_____

Don't Let Them Stop You – It's Personal!

WHAT DOES A HEALTHY RELATIONSHIP LOOK LIKE?

1. Affection

Most healthy couples are affectionate in a good way. They kiss, hug, hold hands, and enjoy cuddling on the couch to watch a movie. This may change a little over time, but if you can't stand to touch each other, that's usually a sign that something is off in your relationship. In a healthy relationship [8], you can have days or weeks where you don't feel like being close physically, but those periods usually pass.

Question:
- When was the last time you passionately kissed your significant other?
- Does one of you tend to cringe or back away from physical contact?
- If you've been drifting apart from each other, did something happen to bring on this change?

2. Trust

Trust is a huge part of healthy relationships. In a healthy relationship, you should be able to tell each other everything, since you know that secrets have their way of coming out eventually. Healthy couples spend time together, but they also have parts of their lives separate from work, hobbies, and spending time with certain friends. That's where trust is extra important.

Ask Yourself:
- Do you trust your significant other? Do they trust you?
- Are you telling any lies in your relationship? If so, why?
- When your significant other does things without you, do you get jealous or suspicious?

Don't Let Them Stop You – It's Personal!

3. Communication

Part of maintaining trust in a healthy relationship requires putting the focus on communication. You need to be able to communicate with your partner if you want your relationship to be healthy. Remember that your partner can't read your mind, even if you think that your feelings should be obvious to them. You need to tell each other how you're feeling if you ever want to get along.

Ask Yourself:
- Are you comfortable telling your significant other when something good OR bad happens?
- Do you fear judgment or criticism when you open-up about things?
- Do the two of you tend to avoid confrontation?

4. Friendship

If you're in a healthy relationship, you probably consider your partner to be one of your friends, if not, your best friend. Maybe you were friends before you got together, or maybe not, but over time, the two of you have developed a special connection. You know things about each other that no one else does, and sometimes, they seem like the person you're most 'yourself' around.

Ask Yourself:
- Do you enjoy spending time with your significant other?
- Are you an important part of each other's lives?
- Have things suddenly become awkward between you, or do you have nothing in common?

5. Bonding

What do friends and healthy couples do? They bond! If you want a relationship that's strong like glue, you need to spend time together and nurture your connection. Even when things are busy, you should take the time to check in with each other at least once a day. Couples in healthy relationships remember to plan dates and solo time together and make plans 'together' with other people.

Ask Yourself:
- When was the last time you made spending time together a priority?
- What are your favourite things to do together?
- Do you always seem to argue when you try to do things as a couple or with friends?

6. Commitment

When someone has cheated in a lot of relationships in the past, it can be hard for them to stop the pattern. You might think that you can make them change, but these habits may have been learned. This means it will take time for them to unlearn those habits if they're willing. For a relationship to be healthy, both people need to be committed and willing to work on any problems that come to the surface.

Ask Yourself:
- Have you talked about your relationship status and agreed not to see other people?
- Do you ever notice your significant other flirting with other people?
- Is commitment something that is important to both of you?

7. Disagreement

Yes, that's right. Disagreement is part of a healthy relationship if it's handled in a certain way. All couples argue or disagree with each other from time to time; that's completely normal. The difference between a healthy relationship and an unhealthy one is that in a healthy relationship, couples can talk through their disagreement and come to a compromise.

Don't Let Them Stop You – It's Personal!

Ask Yourself:
- When you disagree, do you talk about it calmly or do things usually get heated?
- Are you and your significant other able to come to compromises?
- Do either of you hold on to grudges when you don't get your way?

8. Change/Flexibility

A couple of other characteristics of healthy relationships are change and flexibility. If you're in a long-term relationship, you need to be aware that the two of you are going to change over time. You can't assume someone is going to stay the same forever; acting that way can hold a person back. This stops them from growing and becoming their true selves.

Ask Yourself:
- When things change in your relationship, does it cause a lot of tension?
- Does your significant other always bring up things from your past you're trying to put behind you?
- Do you support each other's dreams and goals, even if they change over time?

9. Humour and Fun

When couples fall into a routine where they are consumed by their work and barely make time for each other, the relationship usually suffers. It's important to make time to reconnect and remember why you're working so hard in the first place. When couples forget how to have fun, things get boring. It starts to get difficult being around each other because stress builds up and you don't have an outlet for it.

Don't Let Them Stop You – It's Personal!

Ask Yourself:
- When was the last time you had a good laugh together?
- Do you ever do anything spontaneous and exciting to change things up?
- Are you stuck in a pattern of going to work and staying at home all the time?

DON'T LET THEM STOP YOU!

Is there anything you have just read that reminds you of your current relationship?

_____
_____
_____
_____
_____

What 3 promises do you want to make to yourself after reading this chapter? (I promise I won't look!)

1.
_____
_____
_____
_____
_____

Don't Let Them Stop You – It's Personal!

2.

3.

CHAPTER 5

Bouncing Back From A Setback Is Possible

A "setback" is defined as a slowing of progress: a temporary defeat. Sound familiar? Everyone, without exception experiences setback or "a temporary defeat." I do acknowledge that the degrees of setback and their impact, vary from person to person. Let me state from the outset that this chapter is not designed to minimise anyone's experience, as the impact of life's problems can cause you to feel devasted and even feel that you might not recover!

What's annoying about encountering a setback is it tends to happen just when we believe we are settled or on the cusp of having a season of good times in our lives. The mind is very powerful and inclined to lean towards being fatalistic when negative stuff happens to us (the exceptions to this are the people who have "Pollyanna" syndrome, and everything is sunny no matter what happens!). If you are not familiar with the story of Pollyanna and you like to read, it's a lovely story.

A setback can leave you feeling broken. There's no shame in having these feelings and it's probably best that you acknowledge these feelings before you move on.

There is a multiplicity of situations that can affect individuals, but everything is subjective. What do I mean? Okay, let me give an example; two women may have experienced becoming widows at the same time, and even from the same event; however, based on what their lives were like and how that person processes grief, their feelings and approach to the future may be like night and day!

What might that look like? To break it down even further, one woman might feel she has lost her soulmate and will make inner vows never to open herself to loving anyone else (her rationale: "It's too painful to go through the experience again" and she will remain

Don't Let Them Stop You – It's Personal!

in a state of widowhood for the rest of her life). The other person may feel guilty that she feels sad, but has no intention of living a single life if the opportunity presents itself (her rationale: "Yes, I am upset, but life is for living, and nothing I do will bring him back; I am still here and have my life to live.") Of course, these may appear to be extremes, but for the purpose of the exercise, I wanted to put out a stark example.

Is either one of these individuals giving the wrong responses to their experiences? No, I don't believe so; however, the bigger question is; will your attitude get in the way of your progress?

Now, don't get me wrong, it will be necessary to go through emotional processes when experiencing a setback; however, in order not to get stuck in feelings of perpetual grief (this is also related to loss, not necessarily the physical death of a loved one.)

Where we might consider that losing a loved one is the ultimate setback (and I wouldn't disagree) there are other circumstances and experiences than can delay our sense of progress or moving forward in life.

When looking at setbacks through the lens of culture (and even religion), there are a variety of attitudes that are encouraged to make you feel better.
Some of the more commonly known expressions are:

- "Everything happens for a reason."
- "All things work together for good."
- "What is meant for you is meant for you."
- "This too will pass."

When times are tough, you can be surrounded by people who will either encourage you that things will get better, be dismissive of your situation (or minimise it), or join you in your sorrow. Within some cultures, there are religious practices which encourage the embracing of "karmic" principles. Please note that in the West,

Don't Let Them Stop You – It's Personal!

Karma is considered a negative retribution for the things we have done. This is not an accurate picture of the origin of what karma means (sorry to disappoint some of you!)

In an ideal world, these situations which I am going to talk about (and there may be others that I don't mention), should not change our identity, but they can and sometimes do!

Situations where you are impacted for which the results are out of your control such as:

Losing a job

If you have ever worked and lost your job (even if you weren't really keen on it!) this can have a devasting impact on your life. There are various ways you can end up without a job. This could be for example; through redundancy, retirement, medical retirement, dismissal, or even unfair dismissal.

Oftentimes, you can even find yourself going through the "grief cycle." Others may trivialise these circumstances, but as the saying goes; "He who feels it, know it!" It's easy for people to say "You are not your job," but for people who have built their careers over time, there is a high chance that your sense of identity may well be wrapped up in your work or career.

Is this something you have experienced? _____

Do you believe it has impacted how you see the future?
_____

What action can YOU take to reduce the impact?
_____
_____

Don't Let Them Stop You – It's Personal!

_____

_____

_____

Becoming ill, or diagnosed with a serious illness

This is scary beyond words! No one wants to receive bad news regarding their longevity. Whilst others may sympathise, they cannot be in your shoes, and the experience is owned solely by you. First things first; always put your health as a priority! When you have been diagnosed with an illness, or have become unwell long-term, it is possible that you will have a wide range of emotions including:

- Feeling very angry or frustrated as you struggle to come to terms with your diagnosis – not understanding why it has happened to you, or wondering if this is karma for something you have done asking "What have I done to deserve this?"

- Facing up to your own mortality and the prospect that the illness could potentially be life-ending.

- Worrying about the future – how you will cope, how you will pay for treatment, what will happen to your loved ones, the pain you may face as the illness progresses, or how your life may change.

- Grieving the loss of your health and old life.

- Feeling disempowered to the point of hopelessness, or unable to look beyond the worst-case scenario.

- Regret or guilt about things you've done that you think may have contributed to your illness or injury.

- Shame at how your condition is affecting those around you.

Don't Let Them Stop You – It's Personal!

- Denial that anything is wrong or refusing to accept the diagnosis.

- A sense of isolation, feeling cut off from friends and loved ones who can't understand what you're going through.

- A loss of self. You're no longer you, but rather your medical condition.

How you react emotionally, and the degree of psychological distress you experience depends on many different factors including your age, personality, the type and prognosis of the medical problem you're facing, and the amount of support you have.

Whatever your situation, you should know that experiencing a wide range of difficult emotions is a normal response to a potentially life-changing situation. It doesn't mean you're weak, going crazy, or won't be able to meet the health and emotional challenges that lie ahead.

Is this something you have experienced? _____

Do you believe it has impacted how you see the future? _____

What action can YOU take to reduce the impact?

_____

_____

_____

_____

_____

Don't Let Them Stop You – It's Personal!

Moving home

There is a reason that moving home is in the 5 top stressful events! This is regardless of whether you wanted to move or not, but what if you are in a forced-move situation?

A recent study shows that moving is reported as one of the most stressful life events by individuals around the world. The study indicated that moving was often connected to a plethora of negative mental and physical health risks, so if you are having a hard time adjusting to life in a new place, you are far from alone.

What are the symptoms?

The symptoms of relocation depression may appear similar to those of clinical depression. They include:

- Feeling down or experiencing a persistent low mood
- Feelings of anger or irritability
- Appetite changes
- Weight changes
- Changes in sleep schedule (including insomnia) or energy levels
- Loss of interest in regular activities
- Social withdrawal
- Difficulty completing daily tasks
- Difficulty with personal or sleep hygiene
- Thoughts of suicide.

Don't Let Them Stop You – It's Personal!

Why does relocation depression occur?

Relocation depression can occur due to the stress that moving often causes. Mental burnout is a leading cause of depression, and you may feel this sensation after planning a big move.

Relocation depression might also be caused by the following:

- Losing social connections near your previous home
- Feeling far away from friends and family
- Feeling physically or mentally exhausted from moving
- A disruption in routine
- Fear of uncertainty
- An increased financial burden
- A new job or career opportunity
- Feeling uncertain about your surroundings
- Losing support services in your prior location
- An underlying mental health concern.

While we tend to associate stressors with negative changes in our lives, any change, positive or negative, can lead to stress and heighten your risk for depression. Even if you are excited about living in a new location, the energy of adapting to a new place can wear on you in ways that could lead to mental health challenges. If you think you may be experiencing relocation depression, or an underlying mental health concern, reach out for support.

Don't Let Them Stop You – It's Personal!

Is this something you have experienced? _____

Do you believe it has impacted how you see the future? _____

What action can YOU take to reduce the impact?
_____
_____
_____
_____
_____

Personal relationship breakup

Irrespective of the circumstances which led to the parting of ways, there will invariably be some sense of loss (even if you are very happy about it!). If you were not the one who called time on the relationship, you may you feel extremely rejected, and this experience may have triggered all sorts of anxieties internally. If you were the initiator of the break up, you might have some guilty feelings about no longer wanting your partner.

If you truly both agreed to mutually part, this may feel less painful, but what if you found out that you were being cheated on or lied to about very important matters? This can put a person into an emotional turmoil causing them to doubt who they are and ultimately, harm their self-esteem.

As desperate as we may be to get over a break-up as quickly as possible, it is important to recognise that it may take a while before you are through to the other side.

Don't Let Them Stop You – It's Personal!

After the split, make yourself a priority. There are things you can do to support yourself during this emotionally turbulent time. For example:

- **Give yourself some space** – You don't need to shut your ex out of your life, (but then again, you might need to if the relationship was toxic!); however, you can take some time out from being in contact with them. This will include checking when they were last online!

- **Keep yourself busy** – Take up a new interest or hobby (you might even have a hobby that you gave up spending time with them). Plan activities ahead, meet up with friends and do things that you usually enjoy. You might be on your own, but you can learn to enjoy your own company. Why not do things that you find relaxing like watching a movie, listening to music or playing sport?

- **Talk to your family and friends (only the ones who can support you though!)** – Initially, you may to want to have some time for yourself; however, allow others to support you by helping you to get your mind off things, and can help you get a different perspective. As tempting as it is, try not to use alcohol and other drugs to deal with the pain (yes, I know it's a big ask for some). I am not sanctioning or policing you in your use of substances, but it is worth noting that while going on a bender might help you feel better initially, (not the next morning though!), the after-effects can leave you feeling much worse.

- **Give time to the process of moving on** – Allow yourself time to adapt to the changes after a break-up.

- **Do your best to look after yourself** – Things like eating well, getting enough sleep and staying active. Avoid letting your health run into the ground because you are temporarily feeling unhappy.

Don't Let Them Stop You – It's Personal!

Is this something you have experienced? _____

Do you believe it has impacted how you see the future? _____

What action can YOU take to reduce the impact?
_____
_____
_____
_____
_____

Experiencing or witnessing a traumatic event (PTSD)

It's only in recent times that the condition post-traumatic stress disorder (PTSD) has been recognised to affect individuals outside of being in the military. Here is the most current definition of trauma:

A traumatic event can be:

- A recent, single traumatic event (e.g., car crash, violent assault)
- A single traumatic event that occurred in the past (e.g., a sexual assault, the death of a spouse or a child, an accident, living through a natural disaster or a war)
- A long-term, chronic pattern (e.g., ongoing childhood neglect, sexual or physical abuse)
- A person who has experienced a traumatic event might develop either simple or complex PTSD.

Don't Let Them Stop You – It's Personal!

> **Experiencing a single traumatic event is most likely to lead to simple PTSD**

Complex PTSD tends to result from long-term, chronic trauma and can affect a person's ability to form healthy, trusting relationships.

Is this something you have experienced? _____

Do you believe it has impacted how you see the future?
_____

What action can YOU take to reduce the impact?
_____

_____

_____

_____

Children leaving home

For some people, having your children move home can be a seismic shift in a way that takes them by surprise! Who knew you would miss them so much, to the point that you feel there is a gaping hole in your life? The "empty nest" syndrome is very real for some individuals, and whilst jokes may abound about being glad to have them off your hands, there can be a sense of sadness, even mourning that your parental role is no longer needed.

Is this something you have experienced? _____

Do you believe it has impacted how you see the future?
_____

Don't Let Them Stop You – It's Personal!

What action can YOU take to reduce the impact?

_____

_____

_____

_____

_____

Financial hardship

This is a tough one! The subject of money can be very sensitive and quite right too! Unless you were born into a relatively wealthy background, the chances are you would have had to go out and get a job when you became of age (remember Saturday jobs?) when you had to pay for your bills and living expenses. I have met many people who have fallen on hard times with their finances (me included,) but never met anyone who really wanted to stay there!

Change of circumstances can range from having a reduction in income resulting in struggling to pay your bills, to having to file for bankruptcy due to your level of debt becoming totally unmanageable. Being under financial stress is no joke, whether you feel it is self-inflicted or not. Here in the West, we pride ourselves on having material things e.g., money, nicely furnished house, an apartment, driving a car, being able to go on exotic holidays and eating out at pricey restaurants. That is in essence the summary of the "good life!"

The not-so-subtle message we are being fed via advertising is: "If you manage to acquire all of these things, you will have reached the gold standard of life." Find a millionaire and ask them if this is true; I can almost guarantee that they will laugh (or maybe cry) at the very question!

Don't Let Them Stop You – It's Personal!

Not so much thought is given to saving for a rainy day unfortunately, and whilst it's nice to have stuff, it is also good to think about the future years and get some resources behind you. Nevertheless, regardless of how you got there, when finding yourself in this position it can be a long climb up out of debt and back into a place of financial stability or security. It takes time, patience and probably most importantly, self-discipline.

Maybe you have been financially exploited by someone you truly care for and the pain of being betrayed is greater than the loss of money itself!

We also associate financial exploitation as something that the elderly or those who are highly vulnerable go through, but this does not have to be the case at all. Anyone can become vulnerable to financial abuse and the effects are none the less devasting and hurtful.

Below are some questions you can ask yourself to identify possible signs of financial abuse (this is in no way an exhaustive list):

- Have you noticed unusual or inappropriate transactions on your bank statements?
- Are you unable to access cash, either via banking or income sources, such as your pension or other benefits?
- Are you being pressured into giving your money to others, leaving you without the money you need to pay for essentials?
- Have you recently lost money without any explanation?
- Have you lent money to someone, and they haven't given it back?
- Do you feel pressured or forced into making changes to your will or other financial plans?

If you have been financially exploited or are currently experiencing this, you should seek support immediately.

Don't Let Them Stop You – It's Personal!

Is this something you have experienced? _____

Do you believe it has impacted how you see the future? _____

What action can YOU take to reduce the impact?

_____

_____

_____

_____

_____

Permanently falling out with long term friends

I talked about having friends earlier, but how about when you fall out with them forever? That can feel like the person died, even if they are still alive! As you get older, you usually have less friends, not more, so rebuilding your circle can be a real effort!

Is this something you have experienced? _____

Do you believe it has impacted how you see the future? _____

What action can YOU take to reduce the impact?

_____

_____

_____

_____

_____

Don't Let Them Stop You – It's Personal!

Having to take retirement before you feel ready

How many times did we say: "I can't wait until I get to retire!" Oh, how quickly the years pass by!

Maybe you didn't feel ready to retire; you felt you had more years to give than your employers wanted to give you! Oftentimes, people don't really plan for how they are going to spend their years in retirement. At first, they may feel excited at the prospect of relaxing at home watching TV, and that lasts for about a week, then slowly (or quickly,) it dawns on them about the harsh reality…they are bored!

Our work ethic can be stronger than we realise and are left feeling useless and unproductive. Those who enjoy their retirement usually have a plan, a hobby, pets to look after or something that can keep them occupied during the day (some get roped into looking after the grandkids!) Even with a good plan, you can still feel blindsided by the emotions that start to emerge.

These feelings are more likely to affect you if the majority of your friends were made through your work. Work friends are the folks you interact with socially at the office. Remember these were the people you spent time with during your break, at lunch, or walking to the bus stop together. Every now and then, you may even hang out with them outside of work.

The ceasing of the routine can cause anyone to feel depressed or low. You might find you even miss your line manager, or maybe you worked at the same place as your spouse! Sometimes, people may be given no alternative, but to retire due to health issues and a "medical retirement" is your only option.

The ramifications are that it's all over for you. That's not true because you can medically retire from one job and possibly pick up another one that is not so demanding on your health. Actually, you can do the same with your previous job!

Don't Let Them Stop You – It's Personal!

Is this something you have experienced? _____

Do you believe it has impacted how you see the future? _____

What action can YOU take to reduce the impact?

_____
_____
_____
_____
_____

Setbacks are a part of life; we don't get to choose our setbacks (unfortunately); however, we can learn from them and work through them to find relative success.

You may believe you are the agent of your setback, and I won't lie, that could also be true; but when I last checked, no-one had any angel wings on their backs or halos over their heads! In other words, even when you have set yourself up for a setback, the truth is no-one is perfect, and we all have a past!

DON'T LET THEM STOP YOU!

What 3 promises do you want to make to yourself after reading this chapter? (I promise I won't look!)

1.

_____
_____
_____

Don't Let Them Stop You – It's Personal!

2.

3.

CHAPTER 6

A Word About Spiritual Leaders

This is potentially one of the most complex relationships any individual is likely to encounter, although this will also be based on age of entry, systemic culture, and the dogma (religious beliefs) of the given group. There can be a very fine line between being spiritually led and spiritually abused. The question is, how do you recognise it when you are coming together with a common purpose to spiritually develop yourself?

I think it would be good to define here what is commonly called a "spiritual life" to help those who have not had any interactions with these communities:

Spirituality is often defined as the search for meaning and purpose in life, and the belief in a higher power or force that governs the universe. While spirituality can mean different things to different people, it is often associated with a sense of inner peace, connection, and fulfilment. I think it is worth discussing the benefits of having a spiritual life.

One of the main benefits of having a spiritual life is the sense of inner peace and the calmness it can bring. Many spiritual practices such as meditation, prayer, and mindfulness, are designed to help individuals quiet their minds and find a sense of stillness and tranquility. This can be particularly helpful for people who struggle with anxiety, stress, or other mental health issues.

Spirituality can also provide a sense of purpose and direction in life. By connecting with a higher power or force, individuals may feel a sense of meaning and significance in their lives. This can be particularly important during times of hardship or difficulty, when it can be easy to feel lost or hopeless.

Another benefit of a spiritual life is the sense of connections with others it can provide. Many spiritual practices involve community

Don't Let Them Stop You – It's Personal!

and fellowship, which can help individuals feel a sense of belonging and support. This can be particularly important for people who feel isolated or disconnected from others.

Spirituality can also be a source of strength and resilience during difficult times. By connecting with a higher power or force, individuals may feel a sense of comfort and protection, which can help them cope with adversity and overcome challenges.

Finally, a spiritual life can be a source of personal growth and development. Many spiritual practices involve self-reflection and introspection, which can help individuals identify their strengths and weaknesses, and work towards personal improvement. This can lead to a greater sense of self-awareness and self-acceptance, as well as a deeper understanding of one's place in the world.

Even though I am here to challenge thought processes, there are many benefits to having a spiritual life. Whether it is finding inner peace, a sense of purpose, connection with others, strength during difficult times, or personal growth, spirituality can provide a source of meaning and fulfilment in life. While spirituality can take many forms, it is ultimately about finding a deeper sense of connection with oneself, others, and the world around us.

I am not here to tread on anyone's spiritual toes; I am here to liberate people who feel that they have been emotionally or mentally constrained by the constructs of their spiritual community, to the point that they do not believe they are fulfilling their potential but fulfilling the expectations of others.

In every setting of life, there are good and bad leaders. The spiritual setting is no different. For those of us who have submitted and are immersed in religious communities, it is good for us to examine and be aware of what "Spiritual Abuse" [10] may look like.

Don't Let Them Stop You – It's Personal!

What is spiritual abuse?

Spiritual abuse is characterised by a systematic pattern of coercive and controlling behaviour in a religious context. Spiritual abuse can have a deeply damaging impact on those who experience it.

This abuse may include:

- Manipulation and exploitation
- Enforced accountability
- Censorship of decision making
- Requirements for secrecy and silence
- Coercion to conform [inability to ask questions]
- Control using sacred texts or teaching and the requirement of obedience to the abuser
- The suggestion that the abuser has a 'divine' position
- Isolation as a means of punishment
- Superiority and elitism.

Within safeguarding, spiritual abuse of a child is a form of emotional abuse, and spiritual abuse of an adult is a form of psychological abuse. This distinction is important to ensure that any incidents of spiritual abuse can be addressed within the statutory definitions and categories of abuse that are currently in use, which are different for children and adults.

The key aspect of spiritual abuse is the religious context in which the abuse occurs, and the ways in which people are controlled through the misuse and abuse of religious scripture, divine position, spiritual threats and fear of spiritual consequences, and the suggestion of God as complicit. All or some of these features can be used to control or coerce.

"There are profound consequences to someone who feels unable to comply with abusive behaviour...If you believe that to disagree or to fail to comply, means that you are letting God down or even, in

Don't Let Them Stop You – It's Personal!

extreme cases, that you will not enter heaven, the pressure on you is immense."

Example: Leaders using scriptures or holy writings to induce a religion of fear, performance and bring about compliance.

Does any of what I have mentioned so far sound familiar? I recognise that this may be very difficult for some of you to process because this has become your normal; however, I would recommend that you engage in counselling to support you in extricating yourself from this situation. It's not always easy to walk away from a spiritual community even if abuse is taking place.

What are the key characteristics of spiritual abuse?

Misusing biblical or sacred teachings to coerce behaviour – Behaviour may be coerced through the use of scripture in order to meet the abuser's personal agenda. Biblical messages of submission, sacrifice, obedience and forgiveness can be used to manipulate, control and coerce. The discourses will be recognised by many in the Christian faith and can be healthy and helpful. However, when distorted, they can be difficult to challenge.

Coercing through censorship – This may include pressuring people to secrecy and silence. People may feel unable to ask questions, disagree or raise issues, and this can be associated with the need to keep unity or protect the individual, the Church or God.

Requiring or unquestioning obedience – This may include requiring obedience to the abuser, with an implicit or explicit suggestion that this equates to obedience to God. People may feel unable to make their own choices and can feel pressured into providing financial, emotional and psychological support, service or even sexual activity in order to please their abuser and, it may be implied, to please God.

Using a sense of divine position to exert pressure to conform and suggesting this position is unchallengeable – A spiritually abusive culture/relationship is characterised by a pattern of coercion and control, in which an individual's fear of disobeying God is used to require them to act or adopt a pattern of behaviour without there being free consent.

Enforced accountability – For example, being required to be accountable to another without consent, and without choice and control over boundary setting in the relationship. It should be noted that there are times when accountability is required (for example, where there is a safeguarding agreement), but these are enacted in accordance with the Church of England Policies, Procedures, and Practice Guidance and not as punishment.

Exclusion or isolation of individuals as punishment for non-compliance – An individual may be isolated from others due to perceived non-conformity or disobedience.

Coercing behaviour through exploitation and manipulation – This may include extreme pressure to conform, for example requiring a degree of commitment to attending the place of worship, or the abuser that exceeds what is required of others in the congregation. The level of commitment may be equated to an individual's loyalty to the abuser or to God.

Publicly shaming and humiliating individuals in order to control their behaviour – Individuals may experience public shaming and humiliation because of a perceived lack of obedience or conformity.

Threats of spiritual consequences – This may include exercising control through threats of spiritual consequences for non-compliance with personal directives.

Inappropriate mentoring relationships – The misuse of the pastoral relationship in such a way that the mentor does not hold appropriate boundaries, and justifies this by theology, scripture, or by claiming special spiritual insight or divine sanction.

Don't Let Them Stop You – It's Personal!

What is the impact of spiritual abuse?

As with other forms of abuse, spiritual abuse can result in significant harm to a person. It can also seriously impact a person's faith. As this abuse is a new and emerging area of understanding and is, in fact, often misunderstood and minimised, this can exacerbate the situation. The impact may include:

A. Distrust

Distrust is one of the main consequences of spiritual abuse. Coercion and control can leave individuals unsure of who and what they can trust. It can also lead to a distrust of any believed to be connected to the Christian faith. This could undermine an individual's confidence in any support offered by the Church, including safeguarding and investigation into the abuse.

B. Crisis of faith

Spiritual abuse can lead to damage to, or a loss of faith. The role of faith and scripture in the experience of this abuse can lead individuals to questioning what, if anything, they believe. Individuals who choose to re-engage with a Christian faith may need considerable support to explore scripture for themselves (if they choose to do this), and to understand the misuse of scripture in their own experience.

C. Feelings of powerlessness

As with all forms of abuse, those affected will often feel powerless during the abusive experience and afterwards. They may have felt compelled to be obedient to their abuser and to defer to their decisions. They may struggle to regain control over their lives and may be frightened about doing this.

Don't Let Them Stop You – It's Personal!

D. Feelings of anger and self-blame

People often feel angry about what has happened. The anger can be magnified by the knowledge that it happened in a Christian context, and that scripture and teaching has been used to justify it. People may also blame themselves. They may feel they have been complicit in their abuse or 'allowed' it to take place. They may worry they have unknowingly been complicit in the spiritual abuse of others.

E. Loss of self and identity

For many, faith is central to a sense of self and identity. A loss of faith or loss of a Church role and damaged relationships can result in a direct challenge to this. It may take some time for an individual to build a new positive image of themselves, and it should be recognised that not all individuals may be able to do this where trust has been severely damaged. This is another reason why effective response to abuse is so important.

F. Isolation

Individuals who leave spiritually abusive relationships or environments may find themselves isolated. Other relationships may have diminished due to the effects of the abusive relationship. This may leave the individual with a lack of social support. The distrust experienced can result in deep complexities associated with accessing support and intervention.

Below is a list of scenarios which involve various levels of coercion or spiritual abuse. These are real scenarios which take place within religious settings:

As an exercise, get a pen and cross out either the word "Acceptable" or "Unacceptable."

Don't Let Them Stop You – It's Personal!

Example A of behaviour – Are you in full control of your finances?

- Suggesting that most people could give more if they managed their finances more effectively:
  (Acceptable / Unacceptable)

- It's good for everyone to manage their finances effectively, but have you done your due diligence on the church you're about to give into? Do you have a positive conviction about it?
  (Acceptable / Unacceptable)

- Being overly defensive when speaking to someone who has a different opinion to you on tithing:
  (Acceptable / Unacceptable)

- Pressuring individuals or groups into financial giving:
  (Acceptable / Unacceptable)

- Giving more attention to individuals who are able to give financially:
  (Acceptable / Unacceptable)

- Developing a pattern of defensive and critical conversations with individuals who are unable to give financially:
  (Acceptable / Unacceptable)

- Consistent, intrusive, coercive requests for financial giving suggesting that the level of giving is the most important measure of the individual's commitment to God:
  (Acceptable / Unacceptable)

- The use of biblical scripture to persistently coerce financial giving, or using threats of spiritual consequences to invoke fear if finance is not provided:
  (Acceptable / Unacceptable)

Don't Let Them Stop You – It's Personal!

A persistent pattern of such behaviour would constitute in spiritual abuse. If this was towards a child or a vulnerable adult, this would be considered a safeguarding matter.

Is this something you have experienced? _____

Do you believe it has impacted how you make life decisions? _____

What action can YOU take to change things going forward?

_____

_____

_____

_____

_____

Example B of behaviour – Are you able to ask questions?

- Being overly defensive when asked a question or being challenged respectfully:
  (Acceptable / Unacceptable)

- Not actively listening to a concern:
  (Acceptable / Unacceptable)

- Developing a pattern of defensive and aggressive responses to any question or challenge:
  (Acceptable / Unacceptable)

- Creating a culture in which challenge and questioning are seen as threatening unity:
  (Acceptable / Unacceptable)

Don't Let Them Stop You – It's Personal!

- Regularly suggesting that anyone raising an issue are themselves the issue:
  (Acceptable / Unacceptable)

- A consistent pattern of controlling behaviour suggesting that questioning or challenge is an inability to be obedient to God, and a reflection of a problematic personal faith:
  (Acceptable / Unacceptable)

- Seeking to use Scripture or spiritual threats to close down discussions or silence an individual, rather than to engage with the issues they are raising:
  (Acceptable / Unacceptable)

Is this something you have experienced? _____

Do you believe it has impacted how you make life decisions? _____

What action can YOU take to change things going forward?
_____
_____
_____
_____
_____

Example C of behaviour – Are you being mentored in a healthy way?

- Aiming to be self-reflective and self-aware about one-to-one pastoral conversations:
  (Acceptable / Unacceptable)

Don't Let Them Stop You – It's Personal!

- Being aware of the likely power imbalance in a pastoral mentoring relationship:
  (Acceptable / Unacceptable)

- Possibly having confidential supervision for one-to-one pastoral conversations, or 'checking in' with a third party confidentially about these:
  (Acceptable / Unacceptable)

- Being a little too directive in one mentorship conversation:
  (Acceptable / Unacceptable)

- Being overly defensive when one piece of advice is disagreed with or ignored:
  (Acceptable / Unacceptable)

- Requiring the individual to share personal details which they do not wish to share. Going beyond agreed boundaries:
  (Acceptable / Unacceptable)

- Spiritual mentorship or support becoming very directive and difficult to disagree with, or not comply with:
  (Acceptable / Unacceptable)

- Exploring and interpreting personal psychological history to a depth appropriate to a trained counsellor or psychotherapist:
  (Acceptable / Unacceptable)

- Consistent pattern of highly controlling and directive mentorship:
  (Acceptable / Unacceptable)

- Use of scripture to control behaviour consistently:
  (Acceptable / Unacceptable)

Don't Let Them Stop You – It's Personal!

- Using God's Name to enforce actions the mentor recommends:
  (Acceptable / Unacceptable)

- Making someone feel unable or afraid to disagree with any advice given:
  (Acceptable / Unacceptable)

- Presenting oneself as akin to a professional counsellor, anointed by God for this role with equivalent skills and competencies:
  (Acceptable / Unacceptable)

Is this something you have experienced? _____

Do you believe it has impacted how you make life decisions? _____

What action can YOU take to change things going forward?

_____
_____
_____
_____
_____

Example D of behaviour – Can you set boundaries with your involvement?

- Scheduling a regular meeting on a day that should be the clergy members day off:
  (Acceptable / Unacceptable)

Don't Let Them Stop You – It's Personal!

- Persistently undermining a member of the clergy privately and publicly including commenting on their working hours as a means of undermining them:
  (Acceptable / Unacceptable)

- Consistently using passages of scripture for example, on servant-leadership to control and undermine a member of the clergy to exploit them in demanding excessive working hours with the rhetoric that this is required by God:
  (Acceptable / Unacceptable)

DON'T LET THEM STOP YOU!

Is this something you have experienced? _____

Do you believe it has impacted how you make life decisions? _____

What action can YOU take to change things going forward?

_____

_____

_____

_____

_____

What 3 promises do you want to make to yourself after reading this chapter? (I promise I won't look!)

1.

_____

Don't Let Them Stop You – It's Personal!

2.

3.

CHAPTER 7

Back to you!

With all of what you have read and thought about, you will still have your own life story. First question is: How are you feeling? Second question is: Can you do yourself a (good) favour? My story and experiences will be different to yours. Why? Because in the simplest of terms, we are all individuals with differing backgrounds and cultures. Some of us are more influenced by our culture than others. Those who are from a Caribbean background will share some of my experiences and understand my cultural background of growing up in the UK with Jamaican parents who were also trying to make sense of their brave new world!

Being the child of migrant parents meant that you were likely to have been over-protected, and at the same time, neglected because your parents had to work so hard to pay the bills. It's not easy unless your parents were paid lots of money and flown over first class by a corporate company! Even if that was the case, you were still not exempt from the experiences that acculturation brings!

I was a shy child who spent her head in a book (and not just a few). By the time I was eight or nine years old, I had read most of the Encyclopedia Britannia set my mum had purchased, and my thirst for knowledge really knew no boundaries. I found out many years later that my IQ was quite high and how and mourned what I felt were lost opportunities because I didn't understand my abilities. Then, I got to using my brain! I am both academic and entrepreneurial because my brain allows me to be so (no other reason!) my childhood didn't know this; however, my adulthood does, and I embrace it wholeheartedly!

During my academic studies, I have learned about a very important process called "acculturation" which is relevant to anyone who has had to live in two different cultures at the same time on an ethnicity level. I am going to share this with you because in my humble opinion, it's important.

Don't Let Them Stop You – It's Personal!

ARE YOU HAVING TO STRADDLE TWO OPPOSING WORLDS? YOU ARE IN ACCULTURATION!

Acculturation [11] refers to the process of cultural change that occurs when individuals from different cultural backgrounds come into contact and interact with each other. It is a complex and multifaceted process that involves various aspects of social, psychological, and cultural adaptation. The theory of acculturation attempts to explain how individuals and groups undergo this process and adapt to new cultural environments.

The theory of acculturation has its roots in the study of immigration and the experiences of individuals who migrate to new countries and cultures. It emerged in the early 20th century as sociologists and anthropologists began to study the processes of cultural change that occurred as a result of immigration. The earliest theories of acculturation focused on the idea that immigrants would assimilate into the dominant culture and abandon their own cultural traditions and practices.

However, as research on acculturation continued, scholars began to recognize that the process was much more complex and varied than previously thought. They began to identify various strategies that individuals and groups used to adapt to new cultural environments. One of the most influential frameworks for understanding acculturation is the dual-process model which was developed by John Berry in the 1990s.

The dual-process model proposes that acculturation involves two distinct processes: one, involving the maintenance of the individual's original cultural identity and the other involving the adoption of the new culture. These two processes can occur simultaneously, and individuals can engage in different strategies to navigate them.

The first process, known as cultural maintenance, involves maintaining and preserving one's original cultural identity and practices. This can include maintaining social connections with individuals from the same cultural background, participating in

Don't Let Them Stop You – It's Personal!

cultural practices and traditions, and speaking one's native language. Cultural maintenance is often important for individuals to maintain a sense of belonging and connection to their cultural roots.

The second process, known as cultural adaptation, involves adopting aspects of the new culture and integrating them into one's own identity. This can include learning the language, adopting new cultural practices and customs, and developing relationships with individuals from the new culture. Cultural adaptation is often important for individuals to succeed in the new cultural environment and to be accepted by members of the new culture.

The dual-process model identifies four different acculturation strategies that individuals can use to navigate these two processes: assimilation, integration, separation, and marginalization:

1. **Assimilation** involves abandoning one's original cultural identity and adopting the new culture.

2. **Integration** involves maintaining one's original cultural identity, while also adopting aspects of the new culture.

3. **Separation** involves maintaining one's original cultural identity and avoiding contact with the new culture.

4. **Marginalization** involves rejecting both the original and new cultures and feeling disconnected from both.

Acculturation is a complex and dynamic process that can have significant impacts on individuals and groups. Understanding the theory of acculturation can help individuals and organizations better navigate the challenges and opportunities that arise when different cultures come into contact. By recognizing the importance of both cultural maintenance and cultural adaptation, individuals can develop strategies that allow them to successfully navigate new cultural environments while also maintaining a sense of connection to their cultural roots.

Don't Let Them Stop You – It's Personal!

I hope that the mini discourse above proved helpful to understanding your experiences if you are not in your (or your family's) country of origin.

WE HAVE TO TALK ABOUT SELF-CARE!

Firstly, self-care is not the same as being selfish. Self-care [12] refers to the actions and practices that individuals undertake to maintain and improve their physical, mental, and emotional well-being. While it may seem like a simple concept, the power of self-care cannot be overstated. Let's explore the importance of self-care and the ways in which it can transform our lives.

One of the key benefits of self-care is that it can help us to manage stress. Stress is a natural part of life, but when it becomes chronic, it can have serious negative effects on our health and well-being. By engaging in self-care activities such as exercise, meditation, and spending time in nature, we can reduce our stress levels and promote relaxation. This, in turn, can help us to feel more energized, focused, and productive.

Self-care can also help us to cultivate a positive self-image. When we take care of ourselves physically, mentally, and emotionally, we are sending a message to ourselves that we are worthy of care and attention. This can help to boost our self-esteem and confidence, which can have a positive impact on all areas of our lives.

Another benefit of self-care is that it can improve our relationships with others. When we are feeling stressed, exhausted, or overwhelmed, it can be difficult to be present for our loved ones. By taking care of ourselves, we can ensure that we have the energy and emotional resources to be there for others when they need us. Additionally, when we prioritize our own well-being, we set an example for others to do the same, creating a positive ripple effect in our communities.

It is important to note that self-care is not a selfish act. When we take care of ourselves, we are better equipped to take care of others and contribute to our communities. Self-care is not a luxury, but a necessity for living a healthy and fulfilling life.

However, self-care is not always easy. It requires discipline, self-awareness, and a willingness to prioritize our own needs. It can also be challenging to carve out time for self-care in our busy lives. But the rewards of self-care are well worth the effort.

The truth is that the power of self-care is undeniable. By taking care of ourselves physically, mentally, and emotionally, we can reduce stress, improve our self-image, and strengthen our relationships with others. Self-care is not a luxury, but a necessity for living a healthy and fulfilling life. It is up to each of us to prioritize self-care in our daily lives and reap the benefits that come with it.

SURROUND YOURSELF WITH POSITIVE PEOPLE (AS MUCH AS YOU CAN!)

Surrounding yourself with positive-minded people is an important aspect of personal growth and development. The people we spend time with have a significant impact on our mental, emotional, and physical well-being. Positive-minded people can uplift and inspire us, while negative-minded people can drain and demotivate us. I cannot emphasise enough importance on surrounding yourself with positive-minded people and the benefits that come with it.

But, how do you do this?

Firstly, surrounding yourself with positive-minded people can help you maintain a positive attitude. It is easy to get bogged down by negative thoughts and emotions, especially during challenging times. However, being around people who have a positive outlook on life can help you see the bright side of things. They can provide you with a fresh perspective and inspire you to keep moving

Don't Let Them Stop You – It's Personal!

forward. Positive-minded people are more likely to find solutions to problems rather than dwelling on the negatives.

Secondly, positive-minded people can help you build your confidence. When you surround yourself with people who believe in you and your abilities, you are more likely to believe in yourself. They can help you see your strengths and encourage you to pursue your goals and dreams. On the other hand, negative-minded people can often bring you down and make you doubt yourself. Being around positive-minded people can help you build resilience and self-esteem.

Thirdly, positive-minded people can improve your overall well-being. Studies have shown that people with positive attitudes are more likely to have better mental health and physical health outcomes. Being around positive-minded people can reduce stress levels, lower blood pressure, and boost the immune system. Additionally, positive-minded people are more likely to engage in healthy behaviours such as exercise, healthy eating, and getting enough sleep. Being around them can encourage you to adopt these healthy habits as well.

Lastly, positive-minded people can help you achieve your goals. When you surround yourself with people who have a positive attitude, they can help you stay motivated and focused on your goals. They can provide you with support, accountability, and encouragement. Positive-minded people are more likely to believe and help you reach your full potential.

Please remember that surrounding yourself with positive-minded people is crucial for personal growth and development. The people we spend time with have a significant impact on our mental, emotional, and physical well-being. Positive-minded people can help us maintain a positive attitude, build our confidence, improve our overall well-being, and achieve our goals. Therefore, it is important to surround ourselves with people who uplift and inspire us, rather than those who bring us down.

Don't Let Them Stop You – It's Personal!

A NOTE FOR THOSE WHO STRUGGLE WITH FEELING GUILTY – A LOT!

Guilt is a common emotion that we all experience at some point in our lives. It is a feeling of remorse or regret that arises when we believe we have done something wrong, or failed to do something that we should have done. Guilt can be a healthy emotion when it motivates us to correct our mistakes or make amends. However, it can also become overwhelming and lead to negative consequences such as anxiety and depression. Living in perpetual guilt is tortuous and to be frank; unhelpful.

Here are some strategies for managing guilty feelings:

The first step in managing guilty feelings is to acknowledge and accept them. Trying to suppress or ignore guilt can lead to it becoming more intense and overwhelming. It is important to recognize that feeling guilty is a normal response to making a mistake or failing to meet our own or others' expectations. By acknowledging our guilt, we can begin to understand why we feel that way and take steps to address it.

The next step is to reflect on the situation that caused the guilty feelings. Ask yourself why you feel guilty and what actions or choices led to this feeling. It may be helpful to write down your thoughts and feelings to gain clarity and perspective. This reflection can help you identify what you could have done differently and what you can learn from the situation.

Once you have identified the source of your guilt, take responsibility for your actions. Apologise if necessary, and make amends if possible. Taking responsibility for your actions can help you feel more in control and empower you to make positive changes.

Another strategy for managing guilty feelings is to practice self-compassion. Be kind and understanding towards yourself. Recognize that making mistakes is a part of being human and that everyone makes mistakes. Treat yourself with the same compassion

Don't Let Them Stop You – It's Personal!

and understanding that you would offer a friend who is going through a difficult time.

It is also important to focus on the present and the future, rather than dwelling on the past. Learn from your mistakes and use them as an opportunity for growth and personal development. Set realistic goals for yourself and take small steps towards achieving them. Celebrate your successes and be proud of yourself for making progress.

Finally, seek support from others. Talking to a trusted friend or family member can help you gain perspective and feel less alone. It can also provide you with valuable feedback and support as you work through your guilty feelings.

In conclusion, managing guilty feelings is an important aspect of emotional well-being. Acknowledge and accept your guilt, reflect on the situation, take responsibility, practice self-compassion, focus on the present and the future, and seek support from others. By using these strategies, you can manage your guilty feelings in a healthy and productive way.

DON'T FORGET TO EMBRACE YOUR CULTURE!

There is no "perfect" culture (sorry!). Culture [13] is an essential component of our identity, as it shapes our worldview, values, beliefs, and behaviours. Embracing your culture means accepting and celebrating the customs, traditions, and practices of one's heritage. It is a process of recognising the unique characteristics and contributions of your culture and integrating them into your daily life.

You don't have to embrace the things you consider to be negative; however, there are still lots of elements you can consider especially if you have moved from one country to another and the cultural values are very different to what you are used to!

Don't Let Them Stop You – It's Personal!

Embracing your culture involves several aspects, including language, food, music, arts, clothing, and social norms. Language is a crucial element of culture, as it facilitates communication and expresses the cultural values and beliefs. Learning and speaking your native language is a powerful way to connect with ones' culture and heritage. Similarly, food is an essential part of culture, and the cuisine of a particular culture is an expression of its history, geography, and traditions. Preparing and eating traditional dishes with family and friends is an excellent way to embrace one's culture and pass it on to future generations.

Music, arts, and clothing are other aspects of culture that express the creativity and diversity of a community. Embracing your traditional music and dance can help you connect with ones' roots and appreciate the artistry and craftsmanship of ones' ancestors. Similarly, traditional clothing is an expression of cultural identity and can be worn to celebrate festivals, weddings, and other cultural events.

Embracing your culture also involves understanding and respecting the social norms and values of ones' community. These norms define the expectations and behaviours of individuals within a community and are shaped by the cultural, religious, and historical context. Respecting these norms is a way of honouring one's culture and demonstrating a commitment to preserving its traditions and values.

Embracing your culture can have several benefits, both personal and societal. On a personal level, it can provide a sense of belonging, pride, and identity. It can also help individuals develop a broader perspective and appreciation for diverse cultures and traditions. On a societal level, embracing ones' culture can foster social cohesion, promote cultural diversity, and strengthen community bonds.

However, embracing your culture does not mean rejecting other cultures or being exclusive. Rather, it is about celebrating ones' heritage while respecting and appreciating the cultural diversity of others. It is about recognising that every culture has its unique contributions, and that a diverse and inclusive society is richer and more vibrant.

In these times, we now recognise that embracing one's culture is a powerful way to connect with your roots, express your identity, and preserve one's heritage. It requires a willingness to learn, appreciate, and celebrate the customs and traditions of one's community. By embracing your culture, individuals can gain a sense of belonging and pride, while also promoting social cohesion and cultural diversity.

A short note on racism: What can you change about people being racist towards you? Nothing actually. I am not trying to minimise its impact; however, you need to recognise that ultimately, those things are out of your control, and you still need to get on with your life, bearing in mind what you can control. I wouldn't (and I don't) get dragged down into the weeds of obsessing about who cannot appreciate your racial identity!

STILL FEELING STUCK?

It is important to know that feeling stuck in life is a common experience that many people go through at some point. It can be a frustrating and overwhelming experience, but it is important to remember that it is possible to take steps to move forward and get unstuck. The good news is, we will discuss the steps you can actively take when you are feeling stuck in life.

The first step is to identify the feeling of being stuck. Ask yourself why you feel this way and what may be contributing to it. It may be helpful to write down your thoughts and feelings to gain clarity and perspective. Once you have identified the source of being stuck, you can begin to explore possible solutions.

The next step is to set goals for yourself. Identify what you want to achieve and create a plan to work towards those goals. Make sure your goals are realistic and achievable, and break them down into

Don't Let Them Stop You – It's Personal!

smaller, manageable steps. This can help you feel more in control and motivated to take action.

Another strategy is to try something new. Doing something outside of your comfort zone can help you to gain new experiences and perspectives, and may lead to new opportunities and connections. This could be something as simple as trying a new hobby or taking a class in something you are interested in.

It is also important to practice self-care (I talked about this earlier, but you may have missed it!) Take care of your physical, emotional, and mental well-being. This may include getting enough sleep, eating healthy food, exercising regularly, and engaging in activities that bring you joy and relaxation. Prioritising self-care can help you feel more energised and motivated to act.

Seeking support from others can also be helpful when you are feeling stuck. Talk to a trusted friend, family member, or professional about what you are going through. They may be able to offer guidance, feedback, and support as you work through your challenges.

Finally, remember to be patient and kind to yourself. Moving forward and getting unstuck takes time, effort, and persistence. Celebrate small successes and be gentle with yourself when you experience setbacks. Remember that setbacks are a normal part of the process and can help you learn and grow.

So please, please remember that feeling stuck in life is a common experience, but it is possible to take steps to move forward and get unstuck. Identify the source of being stuck, set goals for yourself, try something new, practice self-care, seek support from others, and be patient and kind to yourself. By taking these steps, you can begin to create a path towards a more fulfilling and satisfying life. Just because you feel stuck doesn't mean you have to remain there!

Don't Let Them Stop You – It's Personal!

NONE OF THIS IS WORKING??

If you are feeling very distressed or depressed and none of what you have read so far has lifted your mood, and you still cannot see any light at the end of the tunnel, then I would strongly recommend that you speak to your GP or other mental and well-being professional. Sometimes, we just don't have the strength to pick ourselves up or move forward, and that's okay! You certainly won't find any judgement over here!

In a society where we can be quick to minimise our troubles, I believe that mental health is a crucial aspect of our overall well-being. It affects how we think, feel, and behave, and can have a significant impact on our relationships, academic or work performance, and overall quality of life.

Unfortunately, mental health problems are common, with many people experiencing symptoms such as anxiety, depression, or stress at some point in their lives. The good news is that there are many effective treatments and therapies available that can help manage and alleviate these symptoms. Seeking professional support for your mental health is an important step towards achieving better mental well-being.

There are many reasons why someone may choose to seek professional support for their mental health. For some, it may be due to experiencing symptoms that are interfering with their daily life, such as difficulty, concentrating or sleeping, feelings of hopelessness or worthlessness, excessive worry or fear.

For others, it may be due to experiencing a traumatic event that has left them feeling overwhelmed or unable to cope. Whatever the reason, seeking professional support can help individuals better understand their symptoms, develop coping strategies, and improve their overall well-being.

One of the most common forms of professional support for mental health is therapy. Therapy is a type of treatment that involves talking to a mental health professional, such as a psychologist, therapist, or

Don't Let Them Stop You – It's Personal!

counsellor, about your thoughts, feelings, and behaviours. During therapy sessions, individuals can learn new skills and techniques for managing their symptoms, gain insights into their emotions and behaviours, and work towards achieving their personal goals. Therapy can be done in one-on-one sessions or in group settings and can be short-term or long-term depending on the individual's needs.

Another form of professional support for mental health is medication. Medications can be helpful in managing symptoms of mental health conditions such as depression, anxiety, or bipolar disorder. However, it's important to note that medication should not be the only form of treatment and is most effective when used in combination with therapy or other forms of professional support.

In addition to therapy and medication, there are many other forms of professional support that can be helpful for mental health. These may include support groups, mindfulness practices, or other alternative therapies such as art or music. There are many forms of therapies which you could explore.

I am personally a great advocate for receiving therapy. This book is written from a place of having been through the most amazing therapeutic input (it was psychodynamic counselling, if you're curious!) and it greatly contributed to me being able to make significant positive changes in my life.

It was a tough emotional ride at times, but if I did not commit to myself to the process, it is unlikely that I would have been able to achieve what I've done so far. Not due to intelligence (my IQ is about 140), but due to the need to strip away a lot of my fears and make some sense of my life experiences. Many years later, I can put my hand on my heart and say I have zero regrets!

DON'T LET THEM STOP YOU!

What 3 promises do you want to make to yourself after reading this chapter?

Don't Let Them Stop You – It's Personal!

1.

2.

3.

CHAPTER 8

How Do I Self-Reflect? (Bonus Chapter)

How do I self-reflect?

Self-reflection [13a] is the process of introspection; the examination and evaluation of one's thoughts, feelings, and behaviours. It is an art that requires a willingness to look within oneself with honesty and objectivity. Self-reflection is an essential tool for personal growth and development, allowing individuals to gain a deeper understanding of their emotions, beliefs, values, and actions.

The art of self-reflection involves a deliberate and systematic approach to examining oneself. It requires taking the time to slow down and reflect on one's experiences, thoughts, and feelings. This can be done through journaling, meditation, or simply taking a few moments each day to reflect on one's experiences.

Through self-reflection, we can as individuals gain insight into our strengths and weaknesses, our fears and desires, and our patterns of behaviour. This insight can help us make more informed decisions, develop better coping strategies, and cultivate greater self-awareness.

One of the benefits of self-reflection is that it allows us to gain a new perspective on our experiences. When we are caught up in the moment, it can be challenging to see things objectively. Self-reflection allows us to step back and view situations from a different angle, providing us with a fresh perspective and new insights.

Self-reflection also enables us to identify areas for improvement and set goals for personal growth. By examining our actions and behaviours, we can identify patterns that may be holding us back and develop strategies for overcoming these obstacles. We can also set goals.

Don't Let Them Stop You – It's Personal!

As we come to understand that self-reflection is the process of examining and evaluating one's own thoughts, behaviours, and emotions, we can use this as a helpful tool for personal growth, self-awareness and self-improvement. Engaging in self-reflection can help us gain a better understanding of our strengths and weaknesses, as well as identify areas for improvement.

How can we engage in self-reflection?

The first step in self-reflection is to set aside time for introspection. This can be done by finding a quiet and comfortable space where you can be alone with your thoughts. It is important to eliminate distractions, such as electronic devices, television, and other people to allow for deeper reflection.

Once a suitable environment has been established, you can start to reflect on your thoughts, behaviours and emotions. You can ask yourself questions such as "What am I feeling right now?" or "Why did I react that way?" These types of questions can help you to identify your emotions, and gain a deeper understanding of why you react in certain ways.

Another useful technique for self-reflection is *journaling*. Writing down thoughts and emotions in a journal can help you gain insight into your own behaviour patterns. It can also be a helpful way to track progress over time and identify areas where improvement is needed.

In addition to journaling, you can also seek feedback from others. This can be done by asking trusted friends or family members for their honest opinions on certain behaviours or patterns. It is important to approach this feedback with an open mind and a willingness to learn and grow.

Finally, it is important to act based on the insights gained from self-reflection. This may involve setting goals for personal growth or making changes to certain behaviours and habits. It is important to be patient and persistent in this process, as change often takes time and effort.

Don't Let Them Stop You – It's Personal!

I think it's fair to conclude that self-reflection is a powerful tool for personal growth and self-awareness. By setting aside time for introspection, journaling, seeking feedback, and acting, we as individuals can gain a deeper understanding of our own thoughts, behaviours, and emotions. This can lead to greater self-awareness, personal growth, and a more fulfilling life.

CONCLUSION

As much as I would love to cover every single facet of life, it is simply not a task I can take on in this particular book. I have not failed to consider those of you who have faced other issues not specifically written about here. There are those who have faced and experienced severe physical, sexual, mental, and emotional abuse out of which there are many stories yet untold. While I cannot attend to everyone's personal wounds, I want to say thank you for reading this book, and my hope is that even though *everything* cannot be fixed, *something* can be fixed as you move forward!

An even bigger hope is that you will be inspired to share your own stories, thoughts, theories, and ideas just as I have, even though the dream seems far away!

A big shout out to all the survivors of the madness that the world brings to our doorstep, and yet, you keep going, you keep breathing, you keep living. You know that deep within where you are now is different to how you see your future! Well, start as you mean to go on. Don't stop moving, don't stop breathing, don't you ever stop living, don't listen to those who tell you that you can't. This time around though, go out and truly live YOUR best life!

And please…don't forget to spend your precious time with people who value you and think you're simply great!

REFERENCES

[1] Parenting Styles:

- Baumrind, D. (1967). Child care practices anteceding three patterns of preschool behaviour. Genetic psychology monographs, 75(1), 43-88.

- Darling, N., & Steinberg, L. (1993). Parenting style as context: An integrative model. Psychological Bulletin, 113(3), 487-496.

[2] Love Languages:

- Chapman, G. D. (1995). The five love languages: How to express heartfelt commitment to your mate. Northfield Publishing.

- Sprecher, S., & Metts, S. (1999). Development of the Love Attitudes Scale: A short form. Journal of Social and Personal Relationships, 16(6), 757-771.

[3] Enmeshment:

- Bowen, M. (1978). Family therapy in clinical practice. Jason Aronson.

- Carter, R., & McGoldrick, M. (1980). The changing family life cycle: A framework for family therapy. Allyn & Bacon.

[4] Healthy Friendships:

- Bukowski, W. M., Hoza, B., & Boivin, M. (1994). Measuring friendship quality during pre-and early adolescence: The development and psychometric properties of the Friendship Qualities Scale. Journal of Social and Personal Relationships, 11 (3), 471-484.

Don't Let Them Stop You – It's Personal!

[5] Setting Boundaries:

- Baumeister, R. F., & Leary, M. R. (1995). The need to belong: Desire for interpersonal attachments as a fundamental human motivation. Psychological Bulletin, 117(3), 497-529.

- MacDonald, G., Locke, K. D., & Asher, M. (2008). Five types of intrapersonal boundaries: A new conceptualization of personality development. Journal of Personality, 76(4), 805-838.

[6] Co-Dependent Relationships:

- Lancer, D. (2018). Conquering shame and co-dependency: 8 steps to freeing the true you. Hazelden Publishing.

- Beattie, Melody. (1992). *Codependent No More*: How to Stop Controlling Others and Start Caring for Yourself. [Center City, MN]: Hazelden, 1992. APA.

[7] Coercion and Control:

- Felson, R. B., & Outlaw, M. C. (2007). The control motive and marital violence. Violence and Victims, 22(4), 387-407.

- Dutton, D. G., & Goodman, L. A. (2005). Coercion in intimate partner violence: Toward a new conceptualization. Sex Roles, 52(11-12), 743-756.

[8] Living with a Narcissist:

- Campbell, W. K., & Foster, J. D. (2007). The narcissistic self: Background, an extended agency model, and ongoing controversies. In C. Sedikides & S. Spencer (Eds.), Frontiers of social psychology: The self (pp. 115-138). Psychology Press.

Don't Let Them Stop You – It's Personal!

[9] Healthy Personal Relationships:

- Reis, H. T., & Shaver, P. (1988). Intimacy as an interpersonal process. In S. Duck (Ed.), Handbook of personal relationships: Theory, research, and interventions (pp. 367-389). Wiley.

- Gottman, J. M., & Silver, N. (2000). The seven principles for making marriage work: A practical guide from the country's foremost relationship expert. Harmony.

[10] Spiritual Abuse:

- Johnson, E. L., & Van Vonderen, J. (1991). The subtle power of spiritual abuse: Recognizing and escaping spiritual manipulation and false spiritual authority within the church. SP Publishing.

- McFarland, I., & Johnson, J. (2007). The spiritual abuse recovery workbook: A healing journey for survivors of spiritual abuse and other forms of religious trauma. CreateSpace Independent Publishing Platform.

[11] Acculturation:

- Berry, J. W. (1997). Immigration, acculturation, and adaptation. Applied Psychology: An International Review, 46(1), 5-34.

- Sam, D. L., & Berry, J. W. (2010). Acculturation: When individuals and groups of different cultural backgrounds meet. Perspectives on Psychological Science, 5(4), 472-481.

[12] Self-Care:

Neff, K. D., & Dahm, K. A. (2015). Self-compassion: What it is, what it does, and how it relates to mindfulness. In M. Robinson, B. Meier, & B. Ostafin (Eds.), Mindfulness and self-regulation (pp. 121-140). Springer.

Don't Let Them Stop You – It's Personal!

Pines, A. M., Aronson, E., & Kafry, D. (1981). Burnout: From tedium to personal growth. Free Press.

Sood, A. (2016). The Mayo Clinic Handbook for Happiness: A Four-Step Plan for Resilient Living. Da Capo Lifelong Books.

[13] Embracing your Culture:

- Benet-Martínez, V., & Haritatos, J. (2005). Bicultural identity integration (BII): Components and psychosocial antecedents. Journal of Personality, 73(4), 1015-1050.

- Abreu, J. M., & Goodyear, R. K. (2000). Affective, cognitive, and behavioral variables related to ethnic identity development in early adolescence. Journal of Early Adolescence, 20(3), 379-405.

[13a] Self-Reflection:

- Tolle, E. (2004). The power of now: A guide to spiritual enlightenment. New World Library.

- Brown, B. (2018). Dare to lead: Brave work. Tough conversations. Whole hearts. Random House.

- Mezirow, J. (1990). How critical reflection triggers transformative learning. Fostering critical reflection in adulthood: A guide to transformative and emancipatory learning, 1-20.

Don't Let Them Stop You – It's Personal!

FURTHER READING

*** The complexity of family dynamics ***

- Carter, B., & McGoldrick, M. (Eds.). (2011). The expanded family life cycle: Individual, family, and social perspectives. Pearson.

- Walsh, F. (2016). Normal family processes: Growing diversity and complexity. Guilford Press.

- Vangelisti, A. L., & Perlman, D. (Eds.). (2006). The Cambridge handbook of personal relationships. Cambridge University Press.

Definitions and insights into the roles of a mother and a father

- "The Role of a mother: A Historical Perspective" by Stephanie Coontz (1992). This article explores the changing societal perceptions and expectations of mothers throughout history and provides insights into the traditional and evolving roles of mothers. It can be found in the journal Gender & Society.

- "The Role of Fathers in Childhood Development: A Global Perspective" by Malin Bergström, et al. (2018). This research article discusses the importance of fathers in child development, including their influence on cognitive, emotional, and social development. It was published in the journal Fathering.

- "The Role of Fathers in Child Development" by Kyle D. Pruett (2000). This book provides an in-depth examination of the role of fathers in child development, discussing their influence on various aspects of their children's lives, including cognitive, emotional, and social development. It offers practical advice for fathers as well. The book is titled "Fatherneed: Why Father Care Is as Essential as Mother Care for Your Child."

Don't Let Them Stop You – It's Personal!

Dealing with setbacks in life

- Seligman, M. E. P. (2006). Learned optimism: How to change your mind and your life. Vintage.

- Neff, K. D. (2011). Self-compassion: Stop beating yourself up and leave insecurity behind. HarperCollins.

Don't Let Them Stop You – It's Personal!

RESOURCES

Here's a list of organizations that provide support for domestic abuse, bereavement, depression, and spiritual abuse:

1. Domestic Abuse:

  - National Domestic Violence Hotline (USA): 1-800-799-SAFE (7233) or www.thehotline.org

  - Refuge (UK): www.refuge.org.uk

  - Women's Aid (UK): www.womensaid.org.uk

  - National Coalition Against Domestic Violence (USA): www.ncadv.org

2. Bereavement:

  - GriefShare: www.griefshare.org (Provides grief support groups in various locations)

  - The Compassionate Friends: www.compassionatefriends.org (Support for families after the death of a child)

  - Cruse Bereavement Care: www.cruse.org.uk (UK-based bereavement support)

  - National Alliance for Grieving Children: www.childrengrieve.org (Support for grieving children and their families)

Don't Let Them Stop You – It's Personal!

3. Depression:

- National Alliance on Mental Illness (NAMI): www.nami.org (Offers resources and support for individuals with depression and other mental health conditions)

- Depression and Bipolar Support Alliance (DBSA): www.dbsalliance.org (Provides peer support groups for individuals with depression and bipolar disorder)

- Mind: www.mind.org.uk (UK-based mental health charity providing resources and support for depression)

4. Spiritual Abuse:

- Recovering from Religion: www.recoveringfromreligion.org (Support for individuals leaving or recovering from harmful religious experiences)

- International Cultic Studies Association (ICSA): www.icsahome.com (Provides resources and support for those affected by cultic or abusive religious groups)

- Safe Passage Foundation: www.safepassagefoundation.org (Support for individuals transitioning out of high-control religious groups)

Please keep in mind the availability of specific resources may vary depending on your location. It's always a good idea to research local organizations and services that cater to your needs. Here are some general suggestions:

5. Financial Abuse Support:

- National Domestic Violence Hotline: Call 1-800-799-SAFE (7233) or visit www.thehotline.org.

Don't Let Them Stop You – It's Personal!

- Adult Protective Services: Contact your local social services or welfare agency for assistance and guidance.

6. PTSD Support:

- National Alliance on Mental Illness (NAMI): Visit www.nami.org or call the NAMI Helpline at 1-800-950-NAMI (1-800-950-6264) for information and support related to mental health, including PTSD.

7. Financial Hardship Support:

- Local Social Services: Contact your local social services or welfare agency to inquire about available financial assistance programs.

- Non-profit Organizations: Research local non-profit organizations that may provide financial assistance or guidance based on your specific circumstances.

NB: Remember, these are general suggestions, and it's important to reach out to organisations and services that are specific to your location for more accurate and relevant support.

www.ingramcontent.com/pod-product-compliance
Lightning Source LLC
Chambersburg PA
CBHW042115100526
44587CB00025B/4064